Corner tower at Burleigh Castle

THE CASTLES OF THE
HEARTLAND OF SCOTLAND

A guide to castles, castellated houses and mottes in the counties of Clackmannan, Dunbarton, Fife, Kinross, Perth, and Stirling.

Mike Salter

FOLLY PUBLICATIONS

ACKNOWLEDGEMENTS

The illustrations in this book are mostly the product of the author's own site surveys between 1977 and 2006. The plans are mostly reproduced to scales of 1:400, 1:800, and 1:2000. The author also drew the sketches and maps and took the majority of the photographs.

Charles Henderson of Auchtermuchty provided accommodation, advice and help. His are the photographs of Aberuchill, Airdrie, Alloa (p9), Almond, Balcarres, Balwearie exterior, Bamff, Bannachra, Boturich, Cardross, Cleish, Darleith, Drummond, Duke Murdoch's, Edinample, Grange, Hallyards, Invermay, Inverquiech, Kilmahew, Kilmaronock, Lethendy, Logie, Otterston, Pitreavie, Rossdhu, Rumgally, Stobhall (p123), Tulliallan, and Whitefield

Thanks are also due to Max Barfield, who provided word processor facilities and checked the text of the original 1994 edition, Helen Thomas for transport, Alan Sorensen, who took the photographs of Old Leckie and Blairlogie, provided accommodation and information on restorations, and transport for the trips on Loch Lomond. Other thanks are due to a number of owners of castles who provided access and information, particularly the Morris family of Balgonie, and especially the Wright family of Plane for much help and accommodation.

AUTHOR'S NOTES

Like the other books in the series (see list inside back cover) this book is intended as a field guide giving as much information and as many illustrations as possible in a volume small and light enough to be used in the field by cyclists and walkers. There is an emphasis towards providing information on, and illustrations of, lesser known buildings , many of them not adequately descibed elsewhere (or at least not in a small enough book to be portable).

The book is intended to be used in conjunction with the Ordnance Survey 1:50,000 scale maps. Grid references are given in the gazetteers. Codes are used to indicate which buildings can be visited, or at least viewed from the outside, as explained on page 19. Care should be taken when visiting ruins not properly maintained and permission obtained where appropriate (it will rarely be refused to bona fida enthusiasts making a polite request). Owners of habitable buildings will sometimes show enthusiasts round if an appointment is made. Remember to leave gates and monuments as you find them, and to keep dogs on leads.

One of the most difficult tasks for preparing this series of five castle books describing all the castles in Scotland was deciding what boundaries and district names to use in view of the considerable changes made in 1974. In general the old county boundaries and names are used in the books. Of the five volumes this is the one most affected by the changes, with the SW part of Perthshire now in Central Region, and the rest now part of Tayside Region.

Each level of a building is called a storey in this book, the basement or ground level room or rooms being the first storey. Sleeping or storage lofts squeezed under vaults are usually treated as separate storeys. Attics entirely within roof spaces are generally mentioned separately, a building thus being of so many storeys plus an attic.

All measurements quoted in the text and the scales on the plans are metric, since the buildings were measuresd by the author in metres. For those who feel a need to convert to imperial 3m is almost the same as ten feet. Unless specifically stated as otherwise all dimensions are external at or near ground level, but above a plinth if there is one.

ABOUT THE AUTHOR

Mike Salter is 53 and has been a professional author and publisher since the end of 1988. Wolverhampton born and bred, Mike has lived since 1990 in an old cottage beside the Malvern Hills. Apart from measuring and photographing old buildings, his interests include maps, walking, backpacking, geo-caching, railways, board games, morris dancing, folk music festivals and performances as percussionist and dance caller with a ceilidh band.

The entrance to Torwood Castle, Stirlingshire

CONTENTS

Maps and notes on other sites occur at the end of each gazetteer.

INTRODUCTION

The word castle came into use in Britain in the 11th century. It was recognised that the many privately owned defensible residences, with which the followers of William, Duke of Normany had filled England after their conquest of that country in 1066, represented something new both in function and appearance. Strategically positioned castles allowed the new Norman land-owning class to establish their rule over the Saxon populace. Under a new system called feudalism the king granted groups of manors to tenants-in-chief in return for specified annual periods of military service by the tenant and his knights. Tenants in turn gave land to their knights on the same basis.

Feudalism was introduced to Scotland in the time of David I. He ruled Strathclyde from 1107 until 1124 under his brother Alexander I, and then himself ruled the whole kingdom until 1153. David lived much of his early life in England under the capable rule of Henry I and became Earl of Huntingdon as a result of his marriage in 1113. David saw the advantages of feudalism over the system previously customary in Scotland when the king was little more than a noble with a special title, having little power outside his own domain. Imposing the feudal system on Scotland increased the king's power and provided him with a regular army other than what he could raise amongst his own tenants, although the more remote districts remained semi-independant until later in the medieval period. About this time primogeniture, or automatic inheritance by the eldest surviving son of a lord's honours and estates, took the place of older systems under which any adult close male relative with recognised leadership qualities might claim all or part of an inheritance, resulting in perpetual quarrels.

There were strongholds in Scotland before King David's time but they were not referred to as castles. There are two or three sites in Perthshire where early kings are said to have had palaces but only the barest earthworks lacking any real shape or pattern survive. Probably they had groups of free-standing timber-framed buildings within a defensive circuit of a ditch, rampart of earth or drystone, and a stockade. The fortress-residences which existed from early times on the volcanic grags at Stirling and Dumbarton have no early remains. These sites were unsuited to earth and timber defences and the early structures were probably of drystone. In the remoter parts of Scotland there are plenty of remains of drystone fortifications ranging from prehistoric times right up until the 16th century.

Motte at Maiden Castle, Fife

Balcastle Motte

David I brought to Scotland knights who had served him in England. The Barclay family, later of considerable importance in Fife, were descended from an English knight called de Berkeley from the place of that name in Gloucestershire, whilst the Stewarts, kings of Scotland from 1371 to 1688 were descended from the Fitz-Alans, who served David and his successors as hereditary stewards. These knights were given lands upon which they built castles, partly as residences, partly as refuges from the initially hostile native stock, and partly as symbols of status and power. Castles continued to be built in central Scotland almost up to the time of Cromwell's invasion of 1650, although of the three elements of residence, status symbol and fortress, the military element gradually became less important. Before they finally went out of fashion military features became symbolic rather than purposeful, retained because they were associated with lordly rank and power.

The new castles built by David's knights were not of mortared stone. Building such structures required years of peaceful conditions, greater expense, and far more skilled masons than were then available in Scotland. Instead they were hastily erected structures of earth and wood. Commonly earth was dug from a circular ditch and piled within it to form a mound called a motte on which was erected a wooden house or tower forming the lord's residence within a small palisaded court. On one side of the motte, or around it, there might be a base-court or bailey containing a hall, chapel, kitchen, stables, barns, workshops, etc, normally defended by a ditch with a rampart and stockade on the inner side. However, not many Scottish mottes have baileys, and the classic upturned pudding-bowl shaped mound with a quadrangular or horseshoe-shaped bailey on one side so common in England and Wales is lacking in central Scotland, where the number of known mottes is only two dozen or so, many of them now damaged or gone. The timber buildings of these sites have long ago perished, although occasionally stumps or traces of holes made for vertical posts are revealed by excavation. The earthworks vary in shape and size. Whenever possible natural features like spurs, promontories and glacial mounds might be given a minimum of scarping and heightening to produce the required shape. On low lying sites by rivers or marshland ditches might be water-filled either permanently or seasonally.

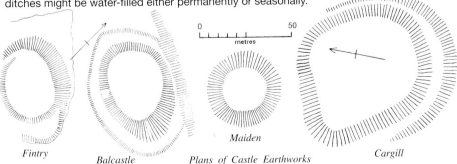

0   50
metres

Fintry

Balcastle

Maiden

Plans of Castle Earthworks

Cargill

Some of the timber buildings on mottes remained in use until the later medieval period, and in the 13th and 14th centuries some lairds had timber manor houses within moated platforms like that at Fortingall in Perthshire. Some of the mottes and flatter, lower, later moated platforms were later refortified in stone but often when a new stone tower was erected it was on a virgin site. There are no secular stone buildings in central Scotland likely to be earlier than 1200, and of buidings generally before the 1360s there are only much rebuilt or very ruined fragments, generally of rather uncertain date. Reliable records of the construction of buildings in this period, and indeed the later medieval period too, are rare in Scotland.

At Kinclaven is a square court which seems to have had corner towers, although not enough remains to indicate their shape or size. Moulin is a smaller and later example of an early courtyard castle with round towers on at least two of the corners. Footings have also been exposed of two round towers of a castle of this type at Falkland. There are very slight remains of originally tower-less courts at Loch Leven and Craigivern. St Andrews has the lower part of a rectangular gatehouse tower of c1200, and it is possible that Macduff's Castle had a stone court and gatehouse by the 1290s. Footings of a court were excavated at Castle Rankine. Aberdour and Blair had early self-contained blocks which probably originally contained just a single fine upper chamber set over a cellar, with the walls rising higher up to enclose the roof. They should thus really be classed as hall-houses rather than towers.

The Scots did not indulge in much castle buildiing during the reigns of Robert I (The Bruce), and his son David II, and most of the castles already existing seem to have been destroyed by one side or the other during Scotland's struggle for independence from England, hence the paucity of both early stone secular buildings and contemporary documents. However, there are some earthworks of this period, namely the ditched platforms on which were built "peles", orginally palisaded courts (the word later came to mean a tower house) serving as easily erected forts during the invasions made by Edward I of England. There are also half a dozen homestead moats, earthworks similar to the peles, but built more for show as status symbols and for keeping wild animals and thieves out of, and domestic animals and servants within, a court around a wooden manor house. These are quite common in parts of England, but only a few can now be traced in Scotland.

There are six 14th century tower houses clustered in Clackmannanshire, Kinross, and the adjacent parts of Fife and Perthshire. Only low fragments remain of Malcolm Canmore's Tower at Dunfermline, but the others all still stand three or four storeys high, and Loch Leven, the least altered, has five storeys. They vary greatly in size, the tower at Dunfermline roughly covering twice the area of Clackmannan, Lochore and Garth. Of these Lochore may be the earliest and has no vaulting. The others all had vaulted basements, and Balgonie has another vault higher up. Vauting increased the structural stability of the towers and helped to resist fire, whether accidental or malcious. Tulliallan is a very different kind of building, a hall-house with two chambers end to end on each of two storeys. The lower storey is rib-vaulted with central piers, a rarity in Scottish secular buildings, and was at least partly for residental or office use. The very ruined island castles of Duke Murdoch's and Inch Murrin seem to have also been hall-houses, but plainer ones with dark basement rooms only suitable for storage.

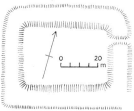

Loop at Newark   *Fortingall: moated site plan*   *Base of a 13th century tower at Falkland*

0   20
m

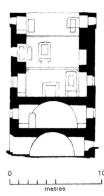

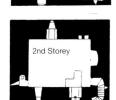

0 ∟⊥⊥⊥⊥∟ 10
metres

*Loch Leven:
plans and section
of tower house*

The main tower at Doune Castle

At Doune, Macduff's, Mugdock and Huntingtower (then called Ruthven), all of c1370 - 1400, the courtyard entrance lay through the base of the principal tower. Mugdock had towers set inside the corners of the court and the same layout appears at St Andrews as rebuilt in this period. There, however, the older gatehouse was converted into a tower house with the entrance passage blocked up, and a new entrance had to be made through the adjacent curtain wall. Doune is the finest and most complete of 14th and 15th century courtyard castles in Scotland, having suffered little damage or alteration. A retainers' hall over cellars and a splendid tower for the lord are grouped together in the form of a screen closing off the naturally weakest side of the court, and on another side is a tower containing a kitchen, itself as big as some of the individual tower houses. Balmbreich has substantial remains of a court of this period with three domestic ranges of differing heights and widths. The three storey range facing the approach originally contained a fine chapel on the middle storey.

Tower houses of the 15th century in central Scotland are numerous, although few survive complete and little-altered. Scottish lords were less wealthy than their English counterparts and had smaller households. A single tower sufficed for their own needs, although there were outbuildings to accommodate retainers, servants and guests within a small court of moderate defensive strength, as seen as Castle Campbell. Because they were more lightly constructed these courts and their buildings were more likely to be partly or wholly rebuilt in later centuries, to fall down through decay, or to be pulled down when gardens and open views from living rooms became the fashion. Of the smaller towers Balmuto, Castle Cary and Plane are fairly complete. Drummond is a square in plan instead of the usual rectangle. Balthayock is exceptionally massive, with two levels of vaults, and may be earlier, as maybe the lower parts of Alloa, whilst Sauchie is notable for its mural chambers and hexagonal caphouse over the spiral staircase. Kilmaronock had mullion-and-transom windows also seen at Doune and Stirling but otherwise rare in Scottish castles. Sometimes a small wing was provided to contain the stair. Usually such a wing would project from a side wall, as at Lordscairnie, but at Pitteadie and Seafield the wing projected from an end wall. Almond and Huntly each have a wing large enough to contain a kitchen with extra private rooms above.

Most of these towers are of four storeys. Where an attic within the wall-walk remains it is usually of later date, although presumably a replacement of the original since the towers seem to have always had gabled roofs. Some towers have entrances at ground level with staircases alongside rising to all levels. Others were entered higher up at hall level and in several instances there are entrances at both levels, sometimes with just a narrow hatch in a vault for hoisting up supplies being the only means of communication between them. The halls often had a screened passage at the end next to the staircase and entrance. The retainers would sit in the cold and dark at this end, the only fireplace being at the other end where the laird and his family had their table. Towards this end the sidewalls end would have windows with seats in the embrasures. Basements were usually vaulted, although in a few instances there was a sleeping loft or retainers' room above, in which case that level would be vaulted to provide a solid floor for the hall, which would thus be on the third storey. The storey above the hall might be just one room but was sometimes divided into a suite of two rooms, one a living room for the laird, and the other his bedchamber. If there was not a mess room below the hall then there might be space for another storey of bedrooms for the laird's family on the top storey. Only if there were five storeys would there be space for both.

Ravenscraig is quite unlike any other 15th century Scottish castle and is the earliest (begun 1460) to have ports for the discharge of firearms. A promontory is screened off by a range with a U-shaped tower at each end, one of which was evidently intended as a self-contained tower house. The other is built up from a much lower level. Of a few years later is the remarkable screen wall built to close off the most vulnerable side of Stirling castle. It consisted of a central gatehouse with drum-towers on all four corners, D-shaped towers set either side of the gatehouse, and walls reaching out to substantial rectangular towers, of which only one still stands above basement level.

Balwearie Castle

West tower at Ravenscraig Castle

Alloa Tower

Balgonie Castle

Added to the earlier tower at Balgonie is a long two storey hall range possibly incorporating part of a second early tower at the far end. Probably of about the same period (the 1490s) is the western wall and SW gate of the courtyard. This, plus the fragments at Lochore, are amongst the earliest surviving examples of such courts being added to tower houses.

Inch Galbraith is a very unusual 15th century island castle. it had a square enclosing wall with a gateway closed by a portcullis. Most of the internal space was taken up with two or three tenement blocks of two storeys leaving only a tiny central court or light-well unroofed.

Rosyth Castle

West tower at Ravenscraig Castle   *Lordscairnie Castle*

In the period 1480 - 1550 parapets often overhang the walls on corbelling. Sometimes this corbelling formed the only decoration on plain buildings with small openings and rubble walls covered with a form of roughcast known to the Scots as harling. Only cut stones used for openings, turrets and corners would be left uncovered. Roundels or shallow open bartizans appear on the corners except for those containing staircases which sometimes had a square gabled caphouse instead. Later in the 16th century roofs are generally brought down directly onto the side walls and the gables are given a series of steps (crowsteps) often rising to a chimney stack. Freestanding chimney stacks were more common in this period since hall fireplaces were now sometimes placed in the middle of a side wall rather than at the laird's end of the hall. Sometimes a topmost storey in the roof has dormer windows with pediments in the side-walls. Often these pediments, and also stones set up over doorways, bear dates, armorial badges, or initials, etc, of lairds and their spouses. They are useful for dating buildings, although some of these stones were simply put up to commemorate weddings, births, inheritances, etc, or when minor repairs or improvements were executed to existing buildings. Also, some of these datestones are not now in their original positions.

On some buildings the roof spaces contained just attic rooms for servants dimly lighted by small windows in the gable-ends. Bartizans now occur in the form of pepper-pot shaped turrets containing tiny closets opening off the topmost rooms and sometimes furnished with shot-holes or gunloops either between or below the windows, or in the decorative supporting coursing. Square bartizans are less frequent but occur at Keltie and Stenhouse. A very common arrangement from the mid 16th century onwards is for turrets containing narrow spiral staircases serving the topmost rooms to be corbelled out above re-entrant angles. Sometimes such turrets occur in the middle of a flat wall-face or on an outer angle. Thus a wing on one side of a main block could contain a wide staircase from the entrance at ground level to the hall on the second storey and then bedrooms above reached by a turret staircase. A common conceit (and an excuse for corbelling, used c1540-1640 as a major decorative feature) is for round towers and turrets to have square caphouses with crow-stepped gables. From 1500 onwards doorways and windows were normally simple rectangular openings sometimes embellished with a moulding. Window tracery was rare. Often only the tops of windows were glazed, the lower parts having wooden shutters (in the medieval period shutters often closed the whole opening), and only in the last few years have restorations begun to reproduce this arrangement.

Kilbryde, Perthshire

Armorial tympanum at Pittarthie, Fife

Gateway at Falkland Palace

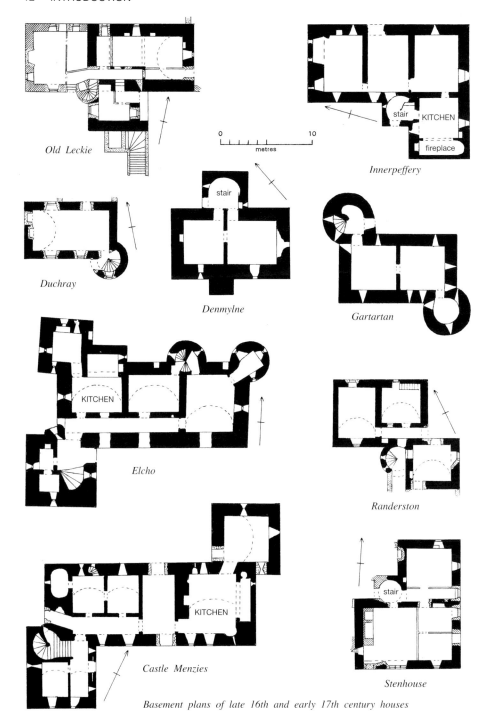

Basement plans of late 16th and early 17th century houses

Newton Doune, Perthshire   *Armorial panel at Leny, Perthshire*   *Doune; waterspout*

Aldie, Bardowie, Burleigh, Culcreugh and Dunmore are examples of plain rectangular early 16th century towers of modest size. The L-plan was very popular throughout the 16th century, Scotstarvit being an example with a wing just large enough to contain the staircase, whilst Cruivie and Balvaird are larger buildings of c1500 with the wings containing kitchens with chambers above.. Balvaird has a square stair turret within the re-entrant angle making a double-stepped L and this layout was repeated somewhat later at Creich and Torwood, although at the latter the wing is used to contain a wide main stair up to the hall. As first built Dairsie was L-planned with a corridor linking two cellars and a kitchen in the basement of the main block to a wide main staircase in the wing. Innerpeffray is an L-planned mansion with a kitchen in the wing. Modified L-plans with the wing flanking two sides of the main block, thus allowing more flanking fire and improved lighting in both parts, occur at Ashintully, Evelick, Whitefield, Randerston and Pittarthie. Duchray has the same idea but with a round tower instead of a wing. Airdrie, Denmylne, Tulliubole and Megginch are T-planned buildings with a stair turret projecting near the middle of one of the long walls. This solved the problem of getting easy direct access to all the bedrooms in buildings where the storeys over the hall were subdivided. Otherwise a subsidiary staircase might be needed to reach the rooms furthest from the main staircase in the wing at one end, as was later provided at Pittarthie. Old Leckie is a T-plan building created by extending the main block of an original L-plan.

More than a dozen towers and mansions conform to the so-called Z-plan where wings or towers project from diagonally opposite corners. Most of the seven castles built between the 1580s and the 1620s by Sir Colin Campbell of Glenorchy were on the Z-plan. Edinample, Gartartan, Inveruglas, and Killernie all have round towers or turrets thus arranged, whilst Grandtully, Finlarig and Menzies have square towers. All-round flanking fire was possible with such a plan if enough gunloops were provided. At Moncur one wing is square and the other is round. Earlshall, Glasclune and Myres are hybrids, being more elongated L-plans with a round tower on the corner diagonally opposite the wing. One end wall at each of these could not be covered by flanking fire. Fordell has a similar layout with both the wing and tower square in plan. Other variations are Fernie, which has a round tower on the outermost corner of an L-plan, Dairsie, an L-plan with round towers added later to opposite corners of the main block, Methven, with round turrets on all four corners, and Elcho, a little-altered mansion still retaining some of its window-grilles and having two square towers at one end, a round turret on a third corner, and another round turret close to it containing a staircase serving rooms at this end beyond a cross-wall. Kellie has ended up with a similar plan but is a composite of three distinct building periods. and several of the other castles contain older work. In the 17th century other plan forms occur, such as the main block with two square wings both on the same side as at Balcomie, Craighall, Pitreavie, and the L-plan with a round stair turret rising the full height of the building within the re-entrant angle, as at Stenhouse.

Royal palace at Stirling

The royal palaces at Stirling and Falkland have plan-forms and architectural details peculiar to themselves. Sir James Hamilton of Finnart was involved with their design and construction. The regular design of the palace facades at Stirling with statues between the windows is classical rather than gothic, one of the earliest works in Scotland influenced by the Renaissance. Only two ranges, one of them ruined, remain at Falkland, along with a gatehouse with twin round towers towards the outside. Stirling is more complete, having four ranges of private apartments around a central court, plus a detached banqueting hall and another block containing a chapel. Another royal palace was gradually formed from the guest ranges at Dunfermline Abbey. Other buildings with ranges around courtyards were Monimail and Duntreath, the latter a composite of many periods from the 14th century onwards. Only a single tower now remains at each of them. Duntreath had a rare detached gatehouse. Stobhall has a court containing several separate modest 16th, 17th and 18th century ranges rather than one large mansion.

Royal palace at Falkland

Cleish Castle, Kinross-shire   *Grandtully Castle, Perthshire*

Internal walls of castles of all periods would be plastered and either painted with biblical or heroic scenes or covered with hangings with similar themes. Fragments of wall paintings survive at Huntingtower. Carpets only became common at the end of the 16th century. Hall floors might be of polished stone slabs if laid on top of vaults but other floors were usually of wooden planks laid on heavy beams and sometimes covered in straw or rushes renewed occasionally. Both ceiling beams and the plaster between them might be painted, again with biblical or heroic scenes, simple patterns, or heraldry. A very fine 17th century heraldic ceiling remains at Earlshall, and another was discovered at Rossend and removed to Edinburgh, whilst another has been re-created in the hall of the tower at Plane. The sash windows which tend to be found in the larger openings of still-inhabited towers and mansions are insertions of the 18th and 19th centuries replacing original narrower openings closed with shutters. Latrines with shutes descending to the foot of the walls are uncommon in post-medieval buildings, having been superseded by the use of chamber-pots.

Window grilles at Elcho, Perthshire   *Bamff, Perthshire*

Pitreavie, Fife

NE tower at Glasclune, Perthshire

There was often a lack of personal privacy in castles. Only the laird and his immediate adult relations would have individual bedrooms. Servants would sleep in dark attic rooms, or perhaps in mural chambers adjoining the main bedrooms. The curtains of four-poster 16th and 17th century beds gave their occupants some privacy. Less than a dozen people might normally reside in a a tower house, although larger mansions like Elcho and Menzies could accommodate many more. Extra servants and guests were often accommodated in outbuildings. Great lords often moved around between seats taking personal servants and some furnishings with them, and thus consumed the produce of their estates in situ. Only a few caretakers might be left when they moved on. Even in the medieval period most castles only had proper garrisons and stocks of munitions in times of unrest.

By the 16th century even the most modest tower would have a walled garden, a dovecot, and an orchard. These are frequently mentioned in 16th and 17th century documents and were then an essential part of the living environment of the landed classes. Sometimes a garden enclosure or dovecot has survived the destruction of the main house or tower. The really great lords also had walled deerparks.

A number of castles were damaged in the conflicts of 1638-54, quite a number being burnt after resisting Cromwell. Only a few castles played any part in the Jacobite rebellions of the 18th century, by which time some had already been left to fall into ruin, whilst others had been modernised and extended. In general 18th and 19th century lairds found dark, cramped old towers inconvenient and often built entirely new houses either in place of, or alongside, the older building. Very few buildings have been allowed to survive both roofed and almost unaltered since the 17th century. Stirling and Dumbarton remained in miltary use until modern times, their defences being updated accordingly. In fact most of the outer defences of both castles are 18th century work with characteristic pepperpot sentry boxes on the corners of ramparts intended to withstand bombardment by cannon.

Bay window of hall at Stirling   *Newton Castle, Perthshire*

About ninety of the 250 odd buildings described in this book are still roofed, including a few which stand empty but complete as ancient monuments. Several have been altered and extended to the point where little remains of any work earlier than the 18th century. Doune and Garth were re-roofed in the late 19th century, and the repair of Menstrie in the 1950s as part of a housing scheme started the current trend towards restoring ruins for private use. Since the 1960s there have been restorations at Balgonie, Balmuto, Couston, Dairsie, Edinample, Old Sauchie, Plane and Pitcullo. Balvaird has been re-roofed by Historic Scotland, and Stirling, Rossend, Garth and Castle Menzies have had recent major internal restorations. On the other hand buildings are still being lost. Since 1960 Skaithmuir and Stenhouse have gone, plus most of Balfour, and half of the upper parts of Dunmore have collapsed.

Bishop's Palace, Dunblane, Perthshire

FURTHER READING

Buildings of Scotland series, volumes for Fife, Glasgow, Stirling & Central Scotland
Historical Castles and Mansions of Scotland: Perth and Forfarshire, A.H.Millar, 1890
Journal of the Perth Society of Natural History (an occasional series)
Medieval Archeology (published annually)
Proceedings of the Society of Antiquaries of Scotland (published annually).
Queen's Scotland series, The Hearland of Scotland, Nigel Tranter, 1971
Royal Commission on Ancient and Historical Monuments: inventories for
    Fife, Kinross & bClackmannan, Stirlingshire, NE Perth.
The Castellated & Domestic Architecture of Scotland, 5 vols D.McGibbon & T.Ross 1880s
The Fortified House in Scotland, 5 vols, Nigel Tranter, 1960s
The Statistical Account of Scotland, edited by John Sinclair, 1790s.
The Scottish Castle, Stewart Cruden, 1960
Scottish Office pamphlets/leaflets for Aberdour, Castle Campbell, Doune, Dumbarton,
    Elcho, Huntingtower, Loch Leven, Ravenscraig, St Andrews, Scotstarvit, Stirling.
The National Trust for Scotland has produced guides for Earlshall and Falkland.
Privately pruduced guides exist for: Blair, Castle Menzies, Drummond, Kellie, Macduff's.

PUBLIC ACCESS TO THE CASTLES

In the gazetteer the names of the buildings are followed by
Ordnance Survey grid references and codes as shown below
to indicate the degree of access or visibility. In practice most
of the buildings can be visited, seen from the outside, or at
least glimpsed in the distance, although permission should
be obtained to approach buildings where there is no obvious
public means of access across private land.

Outer gateway at Scone

A   Buildings now in use as hotels, restaurants, etc.
F   Ruins freely accessible at any time.
G   Grounds or gardens only open to public (a fee may be payable).
HS   Buildings maintained by Historic Scotland where a fee may be payable for access.
NTS   Buildings maintained by the National Trust where a fee is payable for access.
OP   Buildings open to the public by local councils, private bodies. Fee usually payable.
V   Buildings visible from public roads, paths, graveyards, and other public open spaces

Ardross Castle, Fife

A GLOSSARY OF TERMS

Angle-Rounds - Round open bartizans at the corners of a wall-walk.
Ashlar - Masonry of blocks with even faces and square edges.
Attic - A topmost storey entirely within a gabled roof.
Aumbry - A recess or cupboard for storage
Bailey - A defensible space enclosed by a wall or palisade and a ditch.
Barbican - A building or enclosure defending a castle entrance.
Barmkin - An enclosure, usually of modest size and defensive strength.
Bartizan - A turret corbelled out from a wall, usually at the summit.
Berm - A level space between a wall or rampart and the ditch in front.
Caphouse - Small square gabled space over a staircase head or a circular projection.
Commendator - Layman holding abbey revenues in trust when there is no abbot.
Corbel - A projecting bracket supporting other stonework or timber beams.
Crannog - A small artificial island in a freshwater lake which was occupied as a dwelling.
Crow-steps - Square stones forming steps upon a gable.
Curtain Wall - A stone wall enclosing a bailey.
Dormer Window - A window standing up vertically from the slope of a roof.
Gunloop - A small opening suitable for firing pistols or muskets out of.
Gunport - An externally splayed opening suitable for firing cannon or other firearms out of.
Hall House - Two storey building containing a living room over a dark basement.
Harling or Roughcast - Plaster mixed with gravel or other coarse aggregate.
Hoodmould - A projecting moulding above a lintel or arch to throw off water.
Jamb - The side of a doorway, window, or other opening.
Keep - A citadel or ultimate strongpoint. A principal tower. Originally called a donjon.
Lancet - A long and comparatively narrow window usually with a pointed head.
Light - A compartment of a window.
Lintel - A horizontal stone or beam spanning an opening.
Loop - A small opening to admit light or for the discharge of missiles.
Machicolation - A slot for dropping stones or shooting missiles at assailants.
Moat - A ditch, water filled or dry, around an enclosure.
Motte - A steeply-sided flat-topped mound, usually mostly or entirely man-made.
Moulding - A ornament of continuous section.
Mullion - A vertical member dividing the lights of a window.
Oriel - A bay window projecting out from a wall above ground level.
Palace - An old Scottish term for a two storey hall block.
Parapet - A wall for protection at any sudden drop.
Pediment - Low-pitched gable over an end wall or a doorway or window.
Peel - Word originally meaning a palisaded court, later used to mean a stone tower house.
Pilaster - Flat buttress or pier attached to a wall.
Pit Prison - A dark prison only entered through a hatch in the crown of its stone vault.
Plinth - The projecting base of a wall.
Portcullis - A wooden gate designed to rise and fall in vertical grooves.
Postern - A secondary gateway or doorway. A back entrance.
Quoin - A dressed (i.e. carefully shaped) stone at the corner of a building.
Rebate - Rectangular section cut out of a masonry edge usually for a door or yett.
Rere-Arch - An inner arch such as the internal arch over a window or doorway opening.
Respond - A half pier or column bonded into a wall and carrying an arch.
Rib-vault - A vault with ribs below it either for support or decoration.
Scale-and-platt staircase - Staircase with short straight flights and turns at landings.
Shot-hole - A small round hole in an outer wallface for discharging firearms through.
Skewputt - Bottom bracket of a gable upstanding above a roof.
Tower House - Self-contained house with the main rooms stacked vertically.
Tracery - Intersecting ribwork in the uppe parts of a later Gothic window.
Transom - A horizontal member dividing the lights of a window.
Yett - A strong hinged gate made of interwoven iron bars
Wall-walk - A walkway on top of a wall or tower, protected by a parapet.
Ward - A stone-walled defensive enclosure.
Yett - A strong hinged gate made of interwoven iron bars (see picture on page 96).

CASTLES OF FIFE, KINROSS & CLACKMANNAN

ABERDOUR   NT 193854   HS

There is a motte 240m to the north, but the oldest part of the stone castle above the shore is an irregularly set out tower or hall-house probably of c1240-80 measuring 16m by 11m. In the SE side was a doorway and adjacent spiral staircase, plus three loops at ground level and a window composed of twin-lancets above. There was probably only one upper room originally. The east and north corners have clasping pilaster buttresses rising from the plinth. In c1325 Robert I gave Aberdour to his nephew and loyal supporter Thomas Randolpoh, Earl of Moray. His younger son John in 1342 made over the barony to Sir William Douglas. The earliest mention of the castle is in the charter of 1351 by which Sir William granted the lands of Aberdour except the castle to his nephew James, later Lord of Dalkeith. The baronies of Aberdour and Dalkeith were united from 1386 until 1642, the holders having their principal residence at Dalkeith, but also occasionally residing at Aberdour. It may have been James, 4th Lord Dalkeith, who succeeded c1456, and who married James II's sister Joanna and was created Earl of Morton, who rebuilt the upper parts of the tower with ashlar and remodelled the lower part into low cellars with sleeping lofts above. One cellar was subsequently also vaulted. A wing containing a wider staircase than the original staircase was also added.

The 15th century stair-wing was in turn rebuilt when a large new block was added beyond it in the 1570s by George Douglas, 4th Earl of Morton. He served Queen Mary as her Chancellor and was implicated in the murder of her favourite Riccio in 1566. He was Regent for the young James VI from November 1572 until March 1578, and is recorded to have summoned a Privy Council meeting at Aberdour in 1576. He was executed in 1581 on a charge of being party to Lord Darnley's murder in 1567, and his estates were granted to the Earl of Lennox, although they were returned and the act of attainder reversed several years later. The new block is 18m long and contains on each of three storeys two rooms connected by a passageway on the north side adjoining the main stair in wing of the older building. One of the lowest rooms, which are vaulted, is a kitchen. A turret stair adjoining allows direct access from outside to the rooms over the kitchen. Of about the same periood are remains of a bakehouse to the west and the footings of thin walls around a court to the north, with a round turret at the northern corner.

Beyond the 16th century block is a still-habitable two storey range added by William, 6th Earl of Morton, probably when he was Treasurer of Scotland in 1630-36. His initials appear on a gable. By the time of his death in 1648 his fortune had been dissipated in the royal service, the barony of Dalkeith being sold off in 1642. Aberdour thus briefly became the chief seat of the earldom. The gallery on the upper floor of the new wing then contained 46 pictures. The 13th and 16th century blocks are said to have been gutted by fire either in 1689 or 1715, and although rebuilding was considered it was never carried out. By the early 19th century much of the oldest building had fallen. Other parts collapsed in 1844 and 1919.

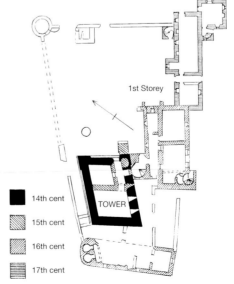

1st Storey

■ 14th cent

▨ 15th cent

▥ 16th cent

▦ 17th cent

TOWER

Plan of Aberdour Castle

Aberdour Castle

Loose window-head at Aberdour

Aberdour Castle   *The oldest parts of Aberdour Castle*

Airdrie Castle

Plan of Alloa Tower

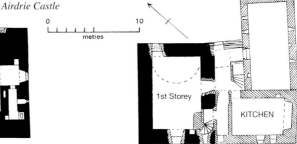

Plan of Aldie Castle

AIRDRIE NO 567084

Airdrie was a barony held by the Lumsden family from at least the mid 15th century until it was sold by Robert Lumsden and his wife Isabel Cor in 1605 to William Turnbull of Pittencrieff. In the 1640s Airdrie was held by John Preston, eldest son of Sir John Preston of Penicuik, whilst in the early 18th century it was held by Philip Anstruther. The building is T-shaped with the wing on the south side bearing the date 1588 and having upper storeys successively corebelled out above those below. The two storey main block measures 24m by 6.3m and has been much altered. It now contains the main stair, although originally there was a stair in the lower part of the wing. Chambers in the wing higher up are reached by a stair in a square turret corbelled out to the west. The hipped roof over the wing is 18th century.

AITHERNIE NO 379035

Only one fragment three storeys high with the jambs of several windows now remain of a late 16th or early 17th century mansion of a branch of the Riggs family of Carbury.

Last remnant of Aitherne Castle

Aldie Castle

Alloa Tower

ALDIE NT 050978

The Mercer family built a four storey tower measuring 10.7m by 8.3m here in the early 16th century. It has a spiral stair in the south corner to the SE of which lay a small wing. This wing rising the full height of the building was later replaced by a longer but lower block containing a spacious living room over a vaulted kitchen with its fireplace in the SE end wall. At the end of 16th century the topmost storey of the tower was rebuilt and provided with new closets in bartizans on the west, north and east corners. At the same time a new wing parallel to the tower was extended out NE of the kitchen block. Blocked doorways suggest a now-destroyed range was also added beyond the NE end of the tower. Soon afterwards most of the tiny court between the original tower and the south wing was filled by a scale-and-platt staircase rising from a new entrance to the upper rooms of the wing and the hall in the tower.

ALLOA NS 889925 NTS

The upper parts of this large tower may date from the 1490s, when it is first mentioned, but the much altered lower two levels may possibly go back to the 1360s, when Sir Robert Erskine served David II as Chancellor. It was the birthplace of John, Earl of Mar, leader of the 1715 Jacobite rebellion. He was forfeited but his son obtained Alloa back in 1739, and until fairly recently it belonged to the Erskine earls of Mar and Kellie. Alloa was in royal hands from 1446 to 1467 after the 1st Lord Erskine fell from favour. The 6th Lord was made Earl of Mar in 1560s. The tower has a low lying site but watchmen on the wall-walk 19m above ground could see the strongholds of Stirling and Clackmannan. The building measures 19.3m by 12.2m wide over walls 3m thick and has four storeys plus an attic. Only the 4th storey retains its original layout of one window embrasure fitted with seats and an aumbry in each wall, a latrine in the east corner, and the spiral staircase in the south corner. Two extra windows on each long side are much later insertions. Part of each of the lower levels is now taken up with a spacious circular staircase. At the summit are very large round bartizans on all four corners and in the middle of the SE side, the latter covering the entrance, which now takes the form of an 18th century classical style doorway. A latrine lies beside the south bartizan. One second storey window to the SW retains its grille. A 17th century wing added on one side has now been entirely removed. See page 9.

Ardross Castle

ANSTRUTHER EASTER   NO 567036   V

The Old Manse is a three storey L-plan house built in 1590, made into a T-plan by adding a wing containing a kitchen and parlour in 1753. It was remodelled in the 1790s and more work was carried out in 1864 and in the 1970s. Dreel Castle, just east of the burn dividing the two Anstruthers, at NO 565035, is no more than a minor fragment of Sir Philip Anstruther's house of 1663.

1st Storey

Plan of Ardross Castle

ARDROSS   NO 509007   F

Excavations on the raised beach 12m above the present shore have cleared out the basement of a 15th century tower 11m long by 8.6m wide over walls 2m and more thick. In the south end wall is the doorway with a straight stair leading off the lobby and there was a service stair in the west wall. The cellar has an aumbry at each end and remains of narrow windows to the east and north. At some period there has been a later building against the north wall. To the south is the basement of a range 27m long by 9.3m wide over walling 1.8m thick, which towards the sea is pierced by the remains of six embrasureas for loops. This range is probably early 16th century and presumably had a hall with chambers at each end on an upper storey. The barony of Ardross was resigned by William de Dishington in 1402 in favour of his son Thomas. In 1607 another Thomas Dishington sold Ardross to William Scot of Elie, and c1690 it passed to Sir William Anstruther of that Ilk. See page 18.

Balcarres

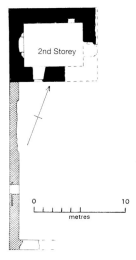

Plan of Arnot Tower

Arnot Tower

ARNOT   NO 207016

Near a modern mansion is a ruined tower 9.7m long by 8m wide over ashlar-faced walls 2m thick with an 18m long section of walling of a former court or later extension adjoining it. The tower was probably newly built in 1507, the date of a charter erecting the lands here into a barony for the Arnot family of that Ilk. David de Arnot held lands here in 1298. A spiral stair in the missing corner connected the vaulted cellar, the hall above, and two upper storeys, Of the hall features there remain a south window and a damaged fireplace in the west wall.

AYTON   NO 302189

A wooden armorial panel survives in one of two recesses on the remaining fragment.

BALCARRES   NO 476044

Much of this large mansion dates from 1838-43 and 1863-7, but it incorporates an L-plan building which may date back to the time of Sir John Fleming, who was granted the estate by James IV in 1511 on condition that he build a house and outbuildings. However the plan form with a round stair turret within the re-entrant angle is more compatable with an account of a house being built here in 1595 by the judge John Lindsay, Lord Menmuir. Possibly he added to an existing structure the rectangular east tower housing a wider stair than that to the west, plus a south wing. Lord Menmuir's grandson Alexander was created Earl of Balcarres by Charles II in 1651. The 3rd Earl began a large new scheme of additions and rebuilding but left only the east wing completed before going into exile because of Jacobite sympathies in 1690. This structure, now detached from the main house, is now called the Dower House. It has lost its upper storeys and has been extended southwards. Alexander, 6th Earl, sold the house to his brother Robert Lindsay of Leuchars in 1791. To the east of the garden lies a ruined chapel in a mixed Gothic and Classical style built in 1635 and having a monogram of David, 1st Lord Lindsay of Balcarres and his wife Sophia.

BALCANQUAL   NO 163010

There are now no remains of a castle probably built c1480 by Archibald Balcanqual.

BALCASKIE   NO 524036

This mansion has been developed from an L-plan house built in the 1620s by the Moncrieffs of Balcaskie. It was of three storeys with the topmost partly in the roof. In 1665 Sir William Bruce purchased Balcaskie and in 1668-74 he extended the building eastwards, heightened it, and provided a four storey NW wing to the older block to match a similar wing on the extension. The new work has much fine plasterwork surviving from this period. In 1684 the house was sold to Sir Thomas Steuart, and in 1698 it was acquired by Sir Robert Anstruther. His son Philip cleared away the original office court and added two pavilions. More alterations were carried out in the 1830s and 1850s.

BALCOMIE   NO 626099

James Learmouth of Clatto was granted Balcomie in 1526 on condition he erect a house, but what remains after considerable alteration and rebuilding c1800 looks somewhat later. It comprised a main block at least 21m long by 9m wide of which only the western third beyond a cross-wall now survives. On the north side by this cross-wall was a turret containing the entrance and main staircase, whilst on the south side were wings which also flanked the end gables. The west wing stands high and has round bartizans now covered by continuations of the main roof, the conical tops having been cut off. Of a court to the north there survives much of the east wall, including a two storey gatehouse with a vaulted porter's room on the north. Over the gateway outer arch are stones with the date 1602 and the initials of John Learmouth and Elizabeth Myrton. There is also the motto "The Lord Bvild The House. They Labour in Vain That Bvild it". There are traces of a former range between it and a later extension to the NE corner of the main block.

Balcomie Castle

Plan of Balcomie Castle

Balfour

BALFOUR   NO 324003

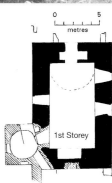

Balfour: plan

The core of this house was a vaulted kitchen within the lowest level of an early 16th century tower measuring 13.3m by 8.6m over walls 1.8m thick. After demolition in the 1980s this room is now all that remains, with traces of a staircase wing added later on the north side. The estate was originally held by the Balfours of that Ilk but passed by marriage to the Beatons. The tower was probably built by John Beaton, for whom a barony of Balfour was created in 1507. Of this family came two Archbishops of St Andrews, Cardinal David Beaton and Cardinal James Beaton. In the late 19th century the estate was sold to Charles Balfour of Balgonie.

Balgonie Castle

Balgonie Castle

BALGONIE   NO 313007   OP

The fine ashlar-faced tower house 20m high to the wall-walk set above a steep bank on the south side of the River Leven was probably built by Sir Thomas Sibbald c1370-80. There are four storeys below the parapet, which was rebuilt in the 16th century. The tower measures 13.3m by 10.6m over walls 2.4m thick. The basement and the hall above are both vaulted and each had its own separate entrance in the east wall, there being no staircase between them, just a hatch in the lower vault. The hall has flues at either end for the smoke from a central fire, and the east end is screened off, as in the original arrangement. A spiral staircase leads up to the laird's hall on the third storey and then to the bedroom above. These top two levels have fireplaces, and latrines are corbelled out of the north wall facing the river.

Balgonie passed by marriage to Sir Robert Lundin, and his son Andrew had work on a hall range east of the tower and a courtyard to the south in progress in 1496, when James IV paid a visit and ordered fourteen shillings to be given to the masons. Of the court of this period there remains the 1.8m thick west wall with corbelling for a parapet. At the south end the wall is thickened by two small guard-rooms. The northerly guard-room has a round outer face with three keyhole-shaped gunloops and a doorway with a drawbar slot gives onto a tiny pit-prison. The hall range is 27.5m long by 9.4m wide over walling as thick as 1.8m on the north and east sides. It contains a long hall with a private room at the east end above three vaulted cellars, one of which is now used as a chapel for wedding services.

Two ceilings in the crow-step gabled two storey SE block are said to have had the initials F.S.A.L for Field Marshal Sir Alexander Leslie, leader of the Covenant Army. He purchased Balgonie from two bankrupt Boswells who had bought the castle from Robert Lundin in 1627. The range must have been built or remodelled by 1641, when Charles I grudgingly made Sir Alexander Earl of Leven. The upper rooms over the vaulted cellars were approached by an external stair from the court. At the same time the hall range was given new upper windows and a third storey with dormer windows and high chimneys was added. A new attic room probably to house a library was added on top of the tower house, the fireplace overmantle having a soldier supporter and the arms used by Sir Alexander after he became an earl. The existing south wall of the court, with a blocked gateway near the east end, is either of this period or the second half of the 16th century, whilst to the south can be seen an outer earthen rampart added to update and strengthen the defences. See pages 9 and 27.

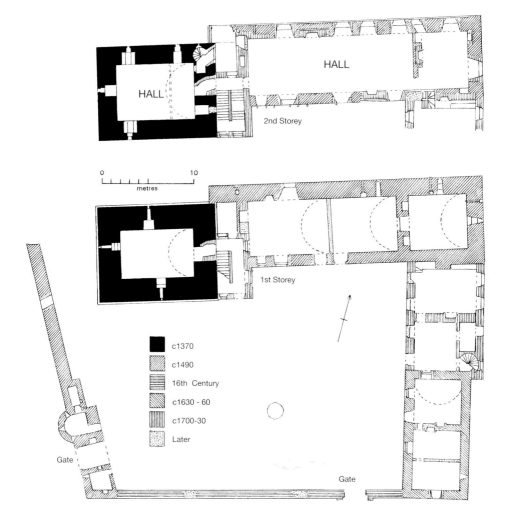

Plans of Balgonie Castle

In 1666 the 7th Earl of Rothes in his capacity as guardian of Margaret, infant countess of Leven, had the apartments repaired and the gap between the tower house and hall block filled with a narrow block containing a scale-and-platt staircase. The three storey block joining the SE range to the east end of the hall block was built in 1706 by the 3rd Earl of Leven, probably on the site of an older range. The castle is said to have been damaged during the Jacobite rebellion of 1715-16, when it was garrisoned by Rob Roy MacGregor, but an inventory of furnishings compiled in 1721 shows it was then quite habitable. The apartments were painted and given sash windows and other improvements in 1755 by David, Lord Balgonie, later 6th Earl of Leven. The castle was sold in 1824 to Sir James Balfour of Whittinghame. He never carried out the intended repairs and by 1840 the building was very decayed. it was sold in 1971 to David Maxwell, who re-roofed the tower house. Restoration is continuing under the present owners the Morris family, who hope to re-roof the other ranges in time.

BALLINBREICH   NO 272205

Overlooking the southern shore of the Firth of Tay are remains of a 14th century courtyard castle of the Leslies. They acquired Ballinbreich (or Balmbreich) in 1312 and later became earls of Rothes. A dukedom was bestowed on the 7th Earl by Charles II in 1680 but that title died with him. A wall about 2m thick enclosed a court which was rectangular but for the NE corner being chamfered off, this part being reduced to footings upon which is a low thin modern wall. A north range facing the sea with important rooms at courtyard level and a basement below has vanished apart from a doorway at the SW corner and the inner wall of a west range has gone. More than half of the south end was filled by a three storey range 9m wide projecting outside the court and thus flanking the original gateway alongside. The middle storey originally formed a chapel with a wide east window, but in the 15th century it was thrown into one with the third storey to make an impressive great chamber with a pointed tunnel-vault. The original sedilia remain behind the southern haunch of this former vault.

The former existence of an iron door-plate bearing the date 1572 with the initials of Alexander, Earl of Rothes suggest that it was he who again drastically remodelled the castle in the late 16th century. A new SE range was added, continuing the alignment of the south range, the junction of the two parts being marked by a D-shaped tower with two tiers of gunports. A new entrance then seems to have been made nearby in the east curtain. The original south range was heightened and remodelled and a staircase turret built in the angle between it and the west range, which was also rebuilt. The southern part of the west range then contained three upper storeys over a kitchen with a fireplace flue projecting beyond the older curtain, but the northern part of the range was only of two storeys. A new north range was built immediatelly south of the original north range, which by then had probably collapsed into the sea. Another staircase turret was provided between it and the west range. Most of these new works are of fine ashlar. In the early 17th century it seems that a two storey block was built against the SE block to form part of the south side of a new eastern outer court of which little now survives.

Ballinbreich Castle

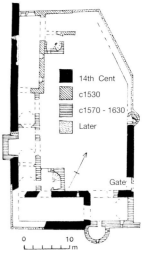

Plan of Ballinbreich Castle

BALMUTO   NT 221898

The castle was restored for a new American owner in 1974-84. It has John Glen's early 15th century tower on the north side, a widened 16th century west range containing a vaulted kitchen, and a two storey south range bearing the date 1594 and initials of John Boswell and Isabella Sandilands. The west range has roll-moulded west windows and has a low modern extension on earlier foundations at the south end. Probably from this range came the lintel with initials of Elizabeth Moncrieff, wife of David Boswell who died in 1582. The Boswells obtained part of the estate of John Glen by marrying a co-heiress but did not obtain the part of the estate including the tower until 1440, when Sir Andrew Ogilvy made it over to David Boswell. The tower measures 9.9m by 7.9m and has on the south side separate entrances into the basement and hall, which were connected by a service stair. Three north windows and two south windows are of 1680, one having a pediment of that date, and another having the initials of David Boswell and Margaret Paterson of Dunmuir. The parapet corbelling is original but the crenellations are of 1787, the period of a doorway now opening to a balcony, but originally towards a range of that period, now demolished.

Balmuto Tower

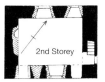

Balmuto: plan

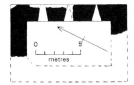

Balwearie: plan

BALWEARIE   NT 252904

This tower was built around 1464, when James III granted William Scot a licence for its construction. It measured 12.9m by 8.4m over ashlar-faced walls 1.8m thick, and contained a cellar and a chamber with a latrine and windows with embrasure seats under a vault, and a hall and two upper storeys above. The western half of the building has gone but the remainder stands 13.5m high to the wall-walk, which had a a parapet on corbels of two members. The hall has one jamb remaining of a south window with a mullion and transom. The fourth storey forming the laird's suite was divided into a small room with a latrine and a larger room with a big fireplace in the east wall. Tusking on the SE corner suggests that there was a court lying to the south and west. See page 8.

Balwearie Castle

Bandon Tower

Bordie

BANDON   NO 277043

Of an early 16th century tower of three storeys and an attic measuring 9.3m by 6.7m there remains the north wall complete up to the parapet corbelling. The round turret alongside formed part of a later court or wing. The tower was built by the Balfours and passed to the Beatons, but from 1580 until 1630 was back in Balfour hands.

BORDIE   NS 955868

Three sides of a late 16th century wing stand high, with a shed built into it. Nothing remains of the main block it was attached to.

BROOMHALL   NT 077837

A house of 1796 lies on the site of the Richardson house of c1580. It was renamed Broomhall after being sold c1605 to Sir George Bruce. His family became earls of Kincardine in 1647.

BURLEIGH   NO 127046   F

Adjoining an early 16th century tower is one surviving wall of a later courtyard with a round-arched gateway and a round corner tower with a still-roofed square caphouse dated 1582 with initials of Sir James Balfour of Mountquhanie and Pittendreich and his wife Margaret Balfour, heiress of the Burleigh branch of the family. Double-splayed gunports in the round tower retain wooden gun-mountings on the sills, and there are circular gunloops higher up. The ruined tower house 9.8m long by 8.2m wide had a hall over a vaulted cellar and two other storeys, plus an attic within a parapet which has mostly fallen, on double-stepped corbels and with angle-rounds. The staircase has been restored as far up as the hall. James VI was a frequent visitor to Burleigh. The Balfours of Burleigh were forfeited after the 1715 Jacobite rebellion. One of them, who took part in the rebellion, had earlier managed to escape in disguise after being sentenced to death for murdering the husband of a woman he loved.

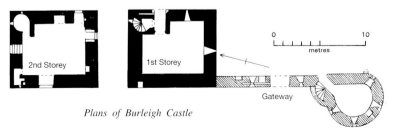

2nd Storey

1st Storey

0   10
metres

Gateway

Plans of Burleigh Castle

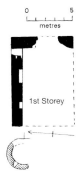

Bandon: plan

Burleigh Castle (see also page 3)

CARDEN NT 227937

High above the Gelly Burn lies the last surviving corner of an early 16th century tower of the Martins of Midhope. The tower was 6.7m wide and had two upper storeys over a basement assumed to have been vaulted. The remaining corner has a round bartizan carried on four continuous moulded courses with gun-loops pointing down towards the ground.

CARSLOGIE NO 353144

The Clephane family held Carslogie for many generations, John Clephane having obtained confirmation of his holding here from Duncan, Earl of Fife in the late 14th century. A stone dated 1710 reset on a shed to the NE of the castle has initials of David Clephane and his wife Joanna Colville. There was once a pediment dated 1590 with initials of George Clephane and Katherine Orme in the ruin, which is probably mostly of that period. It measures 15m by 9m over walling 1.6m thick. The basement contains a central passage between pairs of ash-lar-vaulted cellars each having one loop and one aumbry. A mass of 18th century masonry supporting the foot of a wide circular stair now intrudes into one of the cellars, and part of the passage has been closed off to make a fifth cellar. The large windows of the next storey are 18th century, when a wing, now demolished, was added on the NW side. One window embrasure has a latrine opening off one side and an ogival-headed aumbry in the other. The third storey is very ruined. The building remained occupied until the 19th century.

Carslogie: plan

Carslogie

CASTLE CAMPBELL   NS 962994   HS

Castle Campbell is strongly and beautifully situated on a promontory between the ravines of the burns of Care and Sorrow. The site may originally have been a 12th century motte or ringwork, and a castle here was destroyed in the 1460s by Walter Stewart of Lorne. In the 1480s most of the Glume estate previously divided amongst three Stewart heiresses was obtained by Colin Campbell, created Earl of Argyll in 1457, and he is assumed to have built the tower before his death in 1493. Under James III he served as Master of the Royal House-hold, Justiciar of southern Scotland and Lord High Chancellor, and in 1489, at the start of James IV's minority, he obtained an act of Parliament allowing the name of Castle Glume (or Gloom) to be changed to Castle Campbell. The tower measures 13m by 9m over walls 2.2m thick and rises through four storeys to a parapet on a single row of corbels with tiny angle-rounds. A straight stair rising from the entrance passage connects the basement and com-mon hall, which are both vaulted. The hall has a large fireplace at the east end, and a mural chamber with a hatch to a pit-prison in an adjacent corner. A spiral stair in the SW corner once rose to the lord's hall and bedroom above. These upper rooms each have latrines in the NE corner and mural chambers in or near the SE corner. Both have fireplaces, that of the lord's hall being in the north side wall, and the upper room has a later ribbed barrel-vault.

Castle Campbell became the chief lowland seat of the Earls of Argyll. They frequently resided there until it was burned in 1654 by Royalists in protest against an occupation by Cromwellian troops. In 1566 John Knox is said to have stayed and taught at Castle Camp-bell. Archibald, 8th Earl took a major part in the events of the 1640s and 50s. In 1661 he was executed in Edinburgh for his part in proclaiming Cromwell as Lord Protector. The 9th Earl was executed after leading a Protestant revolt against the Duke of York's rule of Scotland in 1684. The castle was thus not repaired. Inverary was developed as the principal Campbell seat after William III made the 10th Earl a duke in 1689. Castle Campbell was sold by the 6th Duke in the early 19th century. Long overdue repairs carried out in the 1880s included new windows in the east range and new coping on the tower parapet. In 1948 the castle was handed over to the Ministry of Works and the surrounding glen to the National Trust.

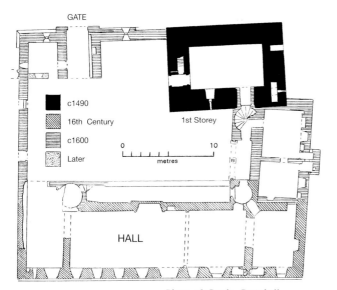

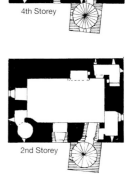

Plans of Castle Campbell

Not long after the tower was built a court was created to the south and west. On the south side was built a range having a hall with two private chambers at the east end over a series of five vaulted cellars set below courtyard level. At the east end there remains one bedroom above reached by a stair in a square turret facing the court and part of the parapet corbelling with one corner roundel. In c1600 this block was linked to the tower house by a still-habitable east range of three storeys and an attic. The narrow tower stair was replaced by a wider one in a turret between the tower and this new block, and a loggia was made between this turret and that of the south range. Of about the same period are the rib-vault of the tower topmost room, the courtyard gateway and adjacent north wall with double-splayed gunports, the inner wall which is all that remains of a former west range, plus the garden terracing to the south.

Old print of Castle Campbell

Castle Campbell

Cleish Castle

Clackmannan Tower

CLACKMANNAN   NS 905920   HS

In the late 14th century Robert Bruce, son of an illegitimate son of King Robert I, built a four storey tower measuring 11.5m by 8.6m. It contained a cellar and sleeping loft below a vault, a vaulted hall above, and a bedroom on top. A straight stair in the west end wall linked the three lower levels and then a spiral stair in the NW corner led up. The middle two storeys were also connected by a hatch in the hall floor. The hall has a fireplace in the west wall and a latrine in the NE corner, and was entered from outside by a door at the east end of the south wall. This doorway now opens into a vaulted kitchen which is the third of six storeys below the machicolated wall-walk of a tall wing added in the 15th century. The topmost storey of the original tower was then rebuilt and another full storey and an attic within a machicolated parapet added on. The parapet and attic on the wing were rebuilt later, and a passage was then driven through the wing to give access from a small court to the east onto the foot of a scale-and-platt staircase up the the hall, this stair being within the western re-entrant angle. The last of the Bruces to occupy the tower was a lady who ceremoniously knighted the poet Robert Burns with the sword of her ancestor who had built the original tower.

CLEISH   NT 083978   V

This lofty five-storey ashlar-faced tower stands on the northern slopes of the Cleish Hills. The main block measures 12m by 9m and there is a wing measuring 6.2m by 8.5m, the end wall of which rises in a series of external offsets. A reset dormer pediment has initials of Robert Colville and Beatrix Haldane with the date 1600, to which period much of the building must belong, but the massively built two lowest levels of the main block are at least a century older. A moulded doorway, now closed, in the re-entrant angle led onto the base of a spiral staircase, now removed, between the main block and the rooms in the end of the wing. A turret stair over the re-entrant angle served the top two storeys. The existing entrance at hall level replaces the original fireplace of the hall and is reached by an external forestair. Along with most of the windows it dates from the 1840s, when the building was restored from a ruinous condition. The main block basement vault was then removed or had already fallen. To the south was a court of which the blocked entrance survives inside a modern outbuilding. See page 15.

COLLUTHIE   NO 340193

Thick older walls remain in a house of the 18th century and later. The castle was built by the Ramsey family, but passed to the Carnegies in 1583, and then went to the Inglis family.

COLLAIRNIE   NO 307170

Little remains of the long low main block, but rising high above a farm steading is the NE wing entered by a doorway with the year 1581 and initials of David Balfour and his wife. The pediment from elsewhere reset in a frame above has the date 1607 and the initials of Henry Balfour. The same date with initials thought to refer to Hugh and David Barclay appear on the tempera-painted ceilings of the third and fourth storey rooms. The attic above originally had dormer windows and closets with gunloops in the bartizans on the eastern corners. There are gunloops at basement level on the north side. A circular turret with an anti-clockwise spiral stair lies within the re-entrant angle. The castle was sold in the early 19th century after the death of the last of this branch of the Barclays.

Cleish Castle

Plan of Clackmannan Tower

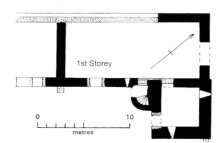

Plan of Collairnie Castle

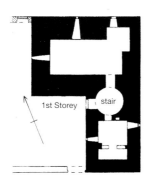

Plan of Cleish Castle

Collairnie Castle

Corston Tower

Cruivie Castle

CORSTON   NO 208098

This late 16th century tower passed from the Ramseys to the Colquhouns in 1669. It measured 8.1m by 6.6m over walls 1m thick and contained three storeys. The west wall containing the entrance with an adjacent circular SW corner stair turret are reduced to the base, but the east wall still stands to its full original height.

COUSTON   NT 168851

This L-planned house beside Otterston Loch was probably built by James Logan after he was confirmed in possession of the estate in 1619. Part of the main block was only two storeys high, the other part having three storeys, and both parts having attics. Until a recent restoration only the wing containing a scale-and-platt staircase and a small later and lower extension adjoining it were still standing in a very ruined state.

CRAIGHALL   NO 407107

The Kinninmonds' mansion was purchased in 1626 by Sir Thomas Hope, Lord Advocate. His son John was raised to the judicial bench as Lord Craighall in 1632. Sir Thomas Bruce Hope transferred to the estate of Kinross inherited from his mother and sold Craighall in 1729. The ruin was demolished in 1955 but drawings and photographs of it survive. The original oblong block had walls up to 3m thick, suggesting a 14th or 15th century date. It was remodelled by the Hopes with two wings on the south side and one on the north which was decidedly off-centre towards the west end. The western wing on the south side had a staircase turret adjoining it. When a screen wall was inserted between the two wings to a design by Sir William Bruce in the 1690s a stair turret was provided to the other wing to balance the design. The east wing bore round bartizans.

CREICH   NO 329212

John Liddall sold Creich in 1502 to David Beaton, son of John Beaton of Balfour. There is uncertainty as to whether the present ruin corresponds to the "castell" here recorded in 1537 but what remains of the corbelling for a parapet with open bartizans on the southern corners suggests possibly a slightly later date. It is an L-shaped building set on a rock, the main block measuring 11.7m by 8.4m and being of three storeys, although the wing contained four. A rectangular turret containing the entrance and staircase lies in the re-entrant angle. The basement contains several vaulted cellars. The round building to the west and the south gable of the 19th century farmhouse may be relics of a surrounding court. In the steading is a lectern-type dovecote dated 1723.

1st Storey

Corston: plan

1st Storey

0 |—|—|—|—|—| 5
metres

Couston: plan in 1984

Creich Castle

CRUIVIE   NO 419229

This massive L-plan tower on a rock was probably newly built in 1509 when Sir James Sandilands of Calder in Midlothian granted to his uncle James Sandilands half of the lands of Cruivie "with the mansion". Sir James' grandfather, who died c1500, had obtained the estate by marrying the heiress of John Kinloch. In 1540 James V granted half of the barony of Cruivie, including the tower, to Henry Ramsey, heir of David Ramsey of Colluthie. Margaret Carnegie, co-heiress of Elizabeth Ramsey, sold her portion of the estate with the tower to her father David Carnegie of Colluthie in 1583. The tower has a wing 7m wide projecting 6.9m from the southern half of the east side of a main block 15m long by 10.4m wide over walls 2.6m thick. The walls stand in a ruinous state 6m high but most of the dressed stones have been torn out and little can be said about the third storey. The entrance was in an unusual position away from the re-entrant angle, being in the north wall at the level of the vaulted second storey. The basement rooms in both main block and wing can only have been reached via hatches in the wooden floors of the second storey. From the entrance a screened passage led across the main block to a doorway to a living room with a fireplace and latrine in the wing. From the north side of this doorway a straight staircase led upwards. The main room at this level was a poorly-lighted retainers' hall or dormitory with two small windows and no fireplace. Above must have been the main hall with a bedroom above it.

2nd Storey

HALL

1st Storey

0 |—|—|—|—|—| 10
metres

1st Storey

Plans of Creich Castle   *Plan of Cruivie Castle*

CULROSS　NS 986862　NTS

The Scottish National Trust maintains two old buildings in this delightful village. The Palace is low lying, of rather irregular layout, and has no defensive features, although the basement is vaulted. It was built by Sir George Bruce in 1597-1611 and passed to the Elphinstones c1700. The other is an L-plan building called The Study which has the topmost room in its wing corbelled out. Yet another old mansion higher up has been created by the Bruce earls of Elgin out of part of the claustral buildings of Culross Abbey.

CUNNINGHAM'S　or　CRAIL　NS 613074

A fragment of a castle of the Spences of Wormiston survived demolition in 1706 and still stood to the east of Crail harbour near Castle Street until the 19th century.

CUPAR　NO 376146

Schoolhill is the site of the early royal castle held by the Macduff earls of Fife in the 13th century. It was captured by Edward I of England in 1296, and was still in use in 1339, whilst courts were held here until 1425. A jail was later built on the site.

DAIRSIE　NO 414160　V

Dairsie belonged to the Learmonth family until 1616, when it was handed over to John Spottiswood, eldest son of Archbishop Spottiswood, the charter mentioning a "manor-place". The Spottiswoods became impoverished by their support for Charles I and by 1647 John had resigned Dairsie to Sir George Morison of Prestongrange, father-in-law of Robert Spottiswood, recently executed along with another kinsman for their part in Montrose's campaign. In the 1990s the ruined castle lying high above the River Eden was restored, the staircase wing and other lost parts being rebuilt of breeze-blocks with a stone outer cladding now covered in harling. The 16th century main block is 17.6m long by 9.3m wide over walls up to 1.8m thick. Added to it probably c1620 are two diagonally opposite round towers with (mostly rebuilt) square caphouses, these parts being of sandstone ashlar, left unharled. The southern tower has three gunports opening from the basement. The NE end contained a private room over a kitchen with a fireplace in the end wall, whilst the rest of the block contained a hall over two vaulted cellars, past which runs a passage between the staircase wing and the kitchen. One of the two wide windows facing SE from the hall has an aumbry in its embrasure, and the other one was later narrowed.

Dairsie Castle as restored

Plan of Denmylne Castle

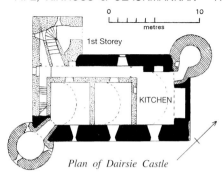

Plan of Dairsie Castle

DENMYLNE   NO 249175

James IV gave Denmylne to John Balfour in c1500 and the present ruin probably dates from shortly after James V gave John's son Patrick a charter of the lands stipulating he must build a hall and offices there. It has a three storey main block 12.4m long by 7.2m wide with a small turret with a solid base projecting from near the middle of the SW side, and a larger turret containing the entrance and staircase near the middle of the NE side. The entrance is covered by two gunports and there are several others in the basement, which is divided into two cellars each having its own doorway from the entrance lobby. The top storey was divided into two bedrooms as one might expect. More unexpected in a tower of this size is the division of the middle storey into a square main hall with a private room to the NW. These rooms have large windows with rounded margins and fireplaces in the end gables. At roof level there was an extra room over the staircase in the wing reached by a narrow stair over the east re-entrant angle and the SE gable and the adjacent part of the NE side as far as the wing have tripple-stepped corbels for a parapet. The wall-walk behind this parapet is thought to have been a pleasant gallery rather than for defence. By the castle is a dovecot with a doorway lintel dated 1706 with initials of Sir Michael Balfour and Dame Marjory Moncrieff.

Dairsie Castle under restoration

Denmylne Castle

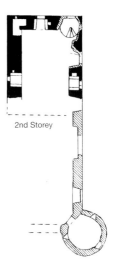

2nd Storey

Dowhill Castle

DOWHILL   NT 118973

This castle of the Lindsays lies on a hill above Loch Leven. It began as a 15th century tower 10.5m long by 8m wide with a staircase in the SE corner linking the adjacent entrance and vaulted cellar with the hall above. The hall has three windows each with seats and aumbries in the embrasures. A latrine chamber in the NE corner has a hatch in the floor to a tiny pit prison fitted with a lamp recess, a urinal, and a ventilation shaft. Nothing remains of the upper storeys. In the late 16th century the tower was remodelled as a "palace" or hall-house, being more than doubled in length. The original entrance was blocked and a new entrance was provided in the base of a stair turret on the north side facing a new barmkin. Of the barmkin only a round turret at the NE corner with one gunloop and several inserted pigeon-nests now survives, and a west range has also vanished except for one out of a series of three cellars connected by a passage fac-

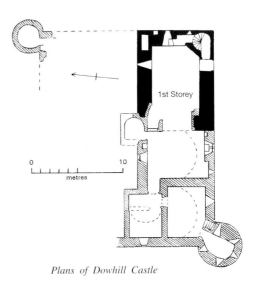

1st Storey

Plans of Dowhill Castle

ing the court. The main block as remodelled contained one cellar on either side of a central kitchen. This kitchen had a huge ireplace in what had been the west wall of the original tower, utilising the flue of the fireplace of the original hall. The western cellar has a service stair leading up in a thickened section of wall in a round SW tower about 5m in diameter diagonally balancing that of the barmkin. The windows of the upper storey have roll-mouldings. The bedrooms above have been destroyed.

Malcolm Canmore's Tower, Dunfermline

Dunfermline Palace

DOWNFIELD   NO 342075

There are ruins of a small tower. Little of interest remains above the vaulted basement.

DUNBOG   NO 285181

One end of the main block of an L-planned building stands complete with a gable, a corbelled-out projection, and an armorial panel high up on the stump of a side wall. Cardinal David Beaton is said to have had a house here. By 1578 it had passed to the Beatons of Creich. The Bannermans are also said to have had a house in this vicinity.

Dunbog

DUNFERMLINE   NT 087873   F

In the park west of the abbey two defaced low walls of a tower at least 17m long by 11m wide lie on a rock perched above the ravine of Tower Burn. It is known as Malcolm Canmore's Tower, and his wife Margaret founded the abbey c1070, although it is unlikely the remains are earlier than the 14th century, by which time the guest range of the abbey had been adopted as a royal palace. The present very impressive ruins are 15th, 16th and 17th century and have no defensive features. Many Scottish monarchs were born here: David II in 1323, James I in 1394, Charles I in 1600 (and his sister Elizabeth, later Queen of Bohemia).

DUNIMARL   NS 976859

To the west of the present picturesque castle-villa built in 1839-45 for Mrs Magdalene Sharpe Erskine is a ruined house built against what is thought to be a section of curtain walling of a medieval courtyard castle. The vaulted structure at the north end of this wall is probably an 18th century icehouse, perhaps within the remains of a tower.

DURIE   NO 372025

The Duries entertained Queen Mary here in 1565. They held this estate from the 13th century until they were forfeited and in 1614 it was sold to the Gibsons, noted lawyers. The Christies' three storey Classical style house of 1762 now stands on the site.

Earlshall Castle

EARLSHALL   NO 465211   NTS

The inscription over the long gallery chimneypiece tells us this Z-plan mansion with a court to the south was begun in 1546 by Sir William Bruce, and completed in 1617 by his great-grandson, another William. The gallery fills the third storey of the main block and has pedimented dormer windows with the arms of Bruce and Lindsay, the latter referring to the later William's second wife Agnes. Their initials and arms and the date 1620 appear on the gallery ceiling, which has painted panels in rows with animals and coats of arms of the great families of Israel, Europe and Scotland. Over the entrance lying at the foot of a staircase turret between the main block and a wing at the west end of the south side are initials of the first Sir William and his wife Margaret Meldrum. The basement has three cellars linked by a passage in the main block, plus a fourth in a round tower projecting from the NE corner, whilst the wing contains the kitchen. There are at this level several dumbell-shaped gunloops. At second storey level the main block has rooms at either end of a fairly short central hall with a fine fireplace on the south side. On the fireplace lintel are arms and initials of Alexander Bruce and Euphame Leslie. They married in 1572 and she died in 1587. The room in the wing at this level has a ceiling with the date 1572 and impaled arms of Bruce and Lindsay.

A screen wall with an arched gateway flanked by gunloops and surmounted by corbelling for a former bartizan links the wing of the main house with a square three storey tower with a stair turret on its northern side. Ajoining this tower and forming the south side of the court is a two storey kitchen range of the 17th century. A still later and narrower block to the east was mostly rebuilt in the general restoration of Earlshall from a derelict state in the 1890s by Robert Lorimer. Originally there were extra bedrooms in a west range which has vanished and just screen walls to the south and east of the court, which contains a well. Eventually a range was added on the east side, but this has been removed, and there is now only a low balustrade on that side. To the SW of the house is a dovecot dated 1599 with initials of Alexander Brice. Earlshall is now administered by the National Trust for Scotland.

EASTER KINNEAR   NO 404232

A 5m high fragment of a tower house of c1600 lies west of Easter Kinnear Farm.

ELIE   NO 488001   V

The castle on the seafront SW of the church is a much-altered 17th century three storey house with a corbelled and crow-stepped gabled caphouse on the wing at the west end of the south side. A kilometre to the NE is Elie House, the oldest parts of which are of c1700, although it is said to be on the site of a castle built in 1366 by Sir Andrew Anstruther.

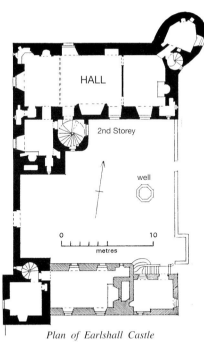

Plan of Earlshall Castle

Earlshall Castle

Elie Castle

FALKLAND   NO 254075   NTS

Of a courtyard castle with round flanking towers built by the earls of Fife in the late 13th century, sloping plinths of good ashlar of the two northern towers partly survive. The castle was captured by Edward III of England in 1337 and supposedly destroyed by him, although it seems more likely to have been dismantled by the Scots after being recaptured. It may not have been rebuilt in its original form but there was a tower house here by 1401 when David, Duke of Rothesay was imprisoned within it. Probably this tower lay on the south side of the original court and it was to the south of this in turn that another court with various buildings was gradually developed by James II and James III, Falkland having been retained by the Crown after the execution and forfeiture of Walter Stewart, Earl of Atholl in 1437.

In 1501 James IV began building a new palace further south. The east range rooms were being plastered in 1506 and were glazed by 1508. A south range containing a chapel over a series of vaulted cellars plus rooms for courtiers, and a north range containing a hall with projecting bays near the east end were built in 1511-13. On reaching adulthood James V resumed the work. He provided a gallery over the east range, remodelled the south range with heavy buttressing towards the outside, and added an impressive gatehouse with twin drum towers at the SW corner. The towers have gunports in their lowest level, heavy grilles on their upper windows and have conical-roofed caphouses within parapets on moulded corbelling. The upper rooms of this gatehouse were designed for the use of the keeper of the palace. The facades of the ranges towards the court were given pilaster buttresses with attached columns on high pedestals. A west range was intended but James V died in 1542 before work upon it started.

The palace was little-used in later years and was described as very decayed in 1598. Some repairs were carried out for Charles I in 1625-9 and the chapel ceiling especially decorated for his five day visit of 1633. Cromwellian troops occupied the palace in the 1650s and managed to set part of it on fire. The north range was subsequently demolished, leaving only footings, and the east range is now roofless and lacking the upper walling on the east side except for a projecting building halfway along called the Crosshouse. Repairs were carried out after Professor John Bruce acquired the palace in 1820, but serious restoration was only undertaken after the 3rd Marquess of Bute took possession in 1887. The National Trust for Scotland has administered the site since 1952. West of the West Loan Burn once lay another castle or old house called Burleigh.

Gatehouse of Falkland Palace

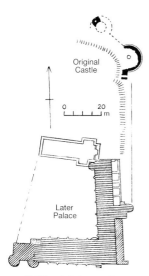

Falkland Palace: plan
(see also pages 6 & 11)

Fernie Castle

FERNIE   NO 316147   A

In 1510 James IV granted Fernie to Florentin Adinulty on condition that he built a "suffi-cientem mansionem" of stone and lime, with hall, chamber, granary, byre, stable, dovecot, orchards, gardens, and bee-phives, with hedges and a plantation of oaks. However before long the Fernies of that Ilk were back in possession and in 1528 the barony of Wester-Fernie was created for Andrew Fernie. The present castle was built in the second half of the 16th century. It has a four storey main block orientated east-west with a staircase wing rising one storey higher set against the west half of the south side, whilst a round tower surmounted by a square caphouse projects from the NW corner. The castle later passed to the Balfours, who added an east extension in the early 18th century. This part was remodelled c1815 for Francis Balfour, when a porch was added in front of the entrance, and a low wing added to the west. Further additions were made in the 1840s and in recent times a round ballroom has been erected in connection with the present usage of the building as an hotel.

FERRYPORT-ON-CRAIG   NT 460290   (approx)

The site of this castle now lies below the high tide level. The lowest storey survived until the local athority had it removed in 1855. It comprised a main block 12m square over walls 2.7m thick with round towers 7.8m in diameter set at diagonally opposite corners. There were two cellars in the main block, each lighted only by a single tiny gunloop, a circular room in one tower, and two oddly shaped rooms in the other tower. These rooms, one of which was a kitchen, each had their own separate entrances from outside and did not communicate with the rest of the building, and in fact an old plan shows no sign of any staircases. In charters of 1588 and 1592 James VI confirmed Robert Melville in possession of the estate. The towers may have been additions of about that period to a main block a century or more older.

Fordell Castle

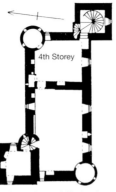

4th Storey

Plan of Fordell Castle

Grange

FORDELL   NT 147854

The Hendersons purchased Fordell in 1511. Over the late 17th century doorway into the heightened NW wing is a broken lintel from elsewhere dated 1580, and an armorial stone dated 1567. It is known that work on a new house for James Henderson was proceeding in 1567, and that it was "brunt by ane suddaine fyre" in 1568. The later stone has initials of James and his wife Jean Murray. It is thought that the castle was originally designed as a shorter block 7.4m wide with a wide staircase in the wing connecting the entrance and a pair of cellars to the hall above, with a stair over the re-entrant angle rising up to two bedrooms over the hall and a third in the wing. A service stair in the SW corner connected the hall and the wine cellar. It seems that after the fire it was decided to lengthen the main block to 16m to provide a private room beyond the hall, with a kitchen below and a fourth bedroom above. A fourth storey providing several more bedrooms was added and round bartizans were provided on the SW and NE corners. These bartizans have gunloops in their corbelling. At the SE corner a square wing flanking both the east and south sides was provided to contain a stair direct from the gardens to the upper rooms. Only later was this stair given an access through to the kitchen. The castle has been little altered externally but in the 1850s the third storey rooms over the hall had their floors removed to make a more lofty chamber with a gallery and a huge chimneypiece was inserted. The floor was reinstated in the 1960s. The house was once surrounded by an outer wall entered via a drawbridge over a ditch. Remains of this wall on the north side were given crenellations in 1856. To the SW is a chapel five bays long dated 1650 over the doorway. The east window is of three lights, and those on the south side are of two lights.

GRANGE   NT 270886

The three storey house incorporates part of an old tower with a round stair turret on one corner. . From the 1540s until it passed to the Melvilles c1739 this was the seat of the Kirkcaldy family. James Kirkcaldy was Treasurer to to James V and his son Sir William was sent to France after being involved in the murder of Cardinal Beaton. He held Edinburgh Castle for Queen Mary in 1571-3, surrendering it on condition he would be unharmed, although he was in fact hanged and forfeited, after which the Douglases held Grange for a short while.

HALLYARDS   NT 212914

Only fragments remain of the late 16th or early 17th century seat of the Skine family. They indicate a court 36m long by 26m wide with traces of a building perhaps of later date in the NE corner, and of a house of two upper storeys over a vaulted basement in the SE corner.

Hallyards

HILL HOUSE   NT 092860

Now hidden inside an addition of 1912 is an entrance into a polygonal stair turret within a re-entrance angle between a main block and a wing. The house was built by William Monteith of Randieford in 1623 and that date appears over the entrance, together with the biblical quote "Woe under him that buildeth his house in unrighteousness".

INCHCOLM   NT 191827   HS

The abbey buildings were partly converted into a dwelling for Henry Stewart, son of the Earl of Moray, for whom the abbey lands were made a lordship in 1611. The island was occupied by the English in 1547 and by French troops in 1548. The island was provided with a gun battery in 1795, and further new batteries during the 1914-18 war.

INCHKEITH   NT 293828

The English government had a fort built here in 1549, supposedly in just two weeks. In the 1550s the site contained a French garrison. A description of 1560 of the defences mentions the ramparts as being 30ft wide, of earth with a stone outer face. The Scottish parliament ordered the fort demolished in 1567 but most of it still existed in 1773 and was not removed until a lighthouse was built in 1803. The present remains comprise a length of walling 48m long and 1.6m thick with gunports and a panel reset on the lighthouse with the year 1564 and the initials M.R. for Maria Regina (Queen Mary).

ISLE OF MAY   NT 658993

After being granted the Isle of May by the Prior of Pittenweem in 1550, Patrick Learmonth remodelled as a residence a building of uncertain purpose orientated north-south. It was perhaps erected after Reading Abbey disposed of its cell here to William, Bishop of St Andrews in the 1270s, and was divided into two, the southern part having an original south doorway later converted into a fireplace with an oven projecting beyond it. The northern part has lancet windows to the west and north. The alterations comprised the insertion of an upper storey without heightening the main block walls, the provision of a now-destroyed block of two unvaulted storeys at the north end, and the adding of a small round tower to the SW corner. The basement of this tower has two gunports flanking the main block and was only reached by a hatch from above.

KELLIE   NO 520052   OP

The Oliphants gained the barony of Kellie from the Siwards in 1361. By the late 15th century they had here a small tower which still survives, and a court which has long since been replaced by a formal walled garden. The L-plan tower now forming the east end of the castle bears the date 1573 and initials of Margaret Hay, who in that year married Laurence, 4th Lord Oliphant. The stone may be reset but it is likely that the tower was built then as a jointure-house for Margaret. There are separate entrances to the tower basement and the staircase in the wing. Higher up the wing contains chambers reached by a stair in a turret over the re-entrant angle. This turret has lost its original conical roof and is now capped by a continuation of the main roof. These upper works, however, probably date from c1603-6 when Laurence, 5th Lord Oliphant built a new main block extending from the west side of the L-plan tower to engage the south side of the 15th century tower, which was then heightened by a new top storey with round bartizans (their conical tops were cut off c1790). On the other side of the new main block a SW tower was added to contain a scale-and-platt stair from the entrance up to the hall, and then three bedrooms above reached by a turret stair over the re-entant angle. The topmost room has dormer windows and closets in round corner bartizans.

The main block contains one large cellar and a service passage below the hall, and a kitchen below the dining room to the east, whilst above are many private rooms. Access to these and to the dining room from the kitchen is facilitated by an additional staircase turret in the middle of the north side. The low extension between this turret and and that of the east tower is a later addition. Pediments over the dormer windows on the south side bear the arms of Lord Oliphant and his wife Lilias Drummond with the dates 1606 and 1724, the latter presumably referring to repairs. Between the towers at the west end is a large crow-stepped gable forming a screen rising above the roof.

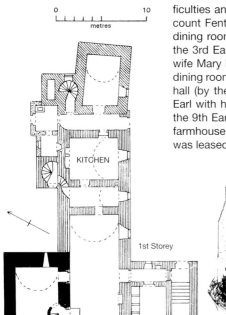

The 5th Lord Oliphant eventually got into financial difficulties and in 1617 sold Kellie to Thomas Erskine, Viscount Fentoun, later created Earl of Kellie. The hall and dining room windows were enlarged just before or after the 3rd Earl returned from exile in Holland with his new wife Mary Kirkpatrick in 1661. Their arms appear on the dining room ceiling. The arms on the plaster ceiling of the hall (by then treated as a drawing room) are of the 3rd Earl with his second wife Mary Dalzell. Kellie passed to the 9th Earl of Mar in 1829 but by then only served as a farmhouse. It was empty and neglected by 1878 when it was leased to and restored by Professor James Lorimer.

Plan of Kellie Castle   *Back view of Kellie Castle*

Kellie Castle

KILCONQUHAR   NO 494027   V

The Bellendens' late 16th century L-plan tower was sold by Adam Bellenden, Bishop of Dunblane to Sir John Carstairs in 1640. In the 18th century the main block was extended eastward. This part was remodelled in the 1830s for Sir Henry Beaton and a large block was added to the north of the original tower. After a fire in 1978 the 18th century wing was mostly demolished and the fourth and fifth storeys of the 16th century tower removed, the stump being roofed as a continuation of the 19th century block to the north. The interior was then divided into flats.

KILLERNIE   NT 033924   V

The castle was built in the late 16th century either by a Scot of Balweary or a Dury of that Ilk, Killernie having been granted in 1540 to Robert Dury after the forfeiture of Sir James Colville of East Wemyss. The building is very ruined but enough survives to show that it had round towers up to 3.8m in diameter furnished with gunloops and set at the NW and SE corners of a main block 12.5m long by 6.5m wide over walls a metre thick. Probably there was a kitchen with a fireplace in the east gable next to the tower containing the staircase and the likely site of the entrance doorway. There are traces of a court to the south with a revetment on the west where the ground falls steeply away. See pages 52 and 53.

KINGHORN   NT 269871

There was a royal castle here in the 12th century, and the town was made a royal burgh by William the Lion. In 1286 Alexander III rode off the nearby cliffs in the dark whilst rushing to join his new wife at the castle. It passed to the Lyons of Glamis in the late 14th century, but all traces of it had gone by 1790. The town, at least, was burned by the English in 1544.

KINGSBARNS   NO 599126

Remains of a castle here survived until the 19th century. It seems to have served as a grain store for the royal palace at Falkland. Not much now remains of the harbour either.

Killernie Castle

Knockdavie Castle

KINKELL   NO 537157

There are now no remains of a castle which fell into decay when a late 17th century owner, Alexander Hamilton, was imprisoned in Edinburgh. It was a ruin by 1767. See page 79.

KIRKTON   NO 458258

The ruined north wall and the round NW tower with one gunport remain of a long mansion. The hall fireplace lintel removed to Kirkton Barns has the date 1585 and arms and initials of David Balfour and Catherine Crichton. The mansion later passed to the Youngs and another stone from it bears the date 1645 with initials of David Young and Elizabeth Nairn. In 1700 Kirkton was acquired by John Gillespie of Newton Rires.

KNOCKDAVIE   NT 213884

This very ruined early 17th century house comprises a main block 20.4m long with a rectangular wing added to the SE corner. The main block was divided into at least three chambers on each storey, the kitchen being at the basement west end. On the north side are a round stair turret and the base of a service stair.

LARGO   NO 418034

A modern panel records that in 1482 Largo was granted by James III to his admiral, Sir Andrew Wood, and in 1491 the latter was given a licence to construct a tower as a defence against pirates, possibly to legalise a structure already built. The lands were erected into a barony in 1513, and in 1618 they passed to Peter Black. in 1633 the latter resigned Largo to the younger Alexander Gibson of Dury, and from his heirs it passed to Sir Alexander Durham, Lyon King of Arms. A new mansion built c1600 was dismantled in the late 18th century leaving only the lower part of the 19m long south wall retained as a boundary, and the conical-roofed round tower 5m in diameter which lay at the SW corner. The tower has a vaulted basement and three upper rooms with roll-and-hollow mouldings around the windows with ornamental quatrefoil gunloops below those at second storey level. External steps now serve the upper levels except for the topmost, which has been made into a dovecot.

LESLIE   NO 259019

Still in use as a retirement home is one very altered range of a palace of the 1670s with four ranges around a court built by the 7th Earl of Rothes. The Leslie family held this estate from the 12th century until modern times, being made peers in 1445, and becoming Dukes of Rothes in 1680. In the garden east of the house are vaulted cellars which once formed part of the north range, and may have been relics of an older house here.

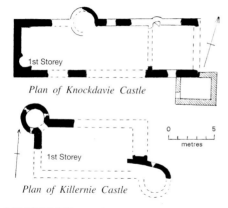

Plan of Knockdavie Castle

Plan of Killernie Castle

LEUCHARS   NO 454220

All that remains is a 12th or 13th century mound 7m high with a summit measuring 95m by 58m. In 1336 the English lords de Beaumont and de Ferrers were in charge of rebuilding, perhaps in stone, of a structure recently destroyed by the Scots. A new building erected in the late 16th century seems to have been on a "palace" plan with a hall and private chamber end-to-end over several cellars. In later years it belonged to the earls of Southesk. Part of the building survived until the late 18th century.

LINDORES   NO 270166 & 266168

A motte lies to the NE of the rocky hillock upon which a later stone castle once stood.

Largo Tower

Loch Leven Castle

LOCH LEVEN   NO 138018   HS

This castle set upon an island in Loch Leven had a stone-built court by the end of the 13th century. In 1335 Alan de Vipont defended the castle against an English force under John de Strivelin sent to take it for Edward Balliol. Robert III is said to have resided in the castle for a while. The Douglas family later had custody of it. Added in the late 14th or early 15th century was the five storey tower house measuring 11m by 9.3m and rising 15.3m to the wall-walk with a plain corbelled parapet with small angle-rounds. It has separate entrances to the vaulted basement and the laird's hall on the third storey, the level inbetween being a vaulted kitchen or garrison mess-room. A spiral stair in the SE corner links the upper levels which have latrines in the SW corner and window embrasures with seats. The fourth storey formed a suite for the lord and there were bedrooms above.

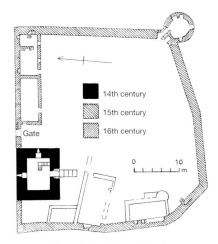

Plan of Loch Leven Castle

The wall of the polygonal court measuring 40m by 38m contains work of several periods, with one thick section probably going back to the 13th century. The round tower and remains of internal buildings, plus slight remains of buildings and an oven outside the NE corner are 16th century. Queen Mary was incarcerated in Loch Leven Castle for most of 1567, during which she signed her abdication, gave birth to still-born twins by her 3rd husband, Francis, Earl of Bothwell, and, with the aid of the Douglas family, made an attempt to escape. The water level of the loch has been lowered, resulting in the island being much bigger than it was previously when the water came up to the walls. See page 54.

Loch Leven Castle

Lochore Castle

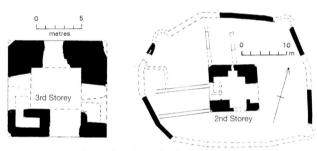

Plans of Lochore Castle

LOCHORE   NT 175959   V

The castle is named after a now-drained loch which still almost surrounded it in the 1780s, and which probably once totally surrounded it. A family of Norman knights took up residence here on a motte in the 12th century, a David de Lochore being mentioned as a magnate in 1255. The lands passed via an heiress to the Valance family, who in the 14th century built a tower of four unvaulted storeys on the truncated motte top. The tower was almost a square of about 10.6m over walls 2.7m thick. The basement is now mostly filled with debris. The entrance in the west wall was at the level of the hall above, which has a fireplace in the north wall and remains of mural chambers in each of the other walls, those to the east and south being reached from window embrasures. The upper levels, now very fragmentary, had chambers, perhaps latrines, in an eastern projection and were connected by a stair in the SW corner. There is no indication of how they were reached from below. Surrounding the motte base are fragments of a barmkin wall 1m thick with one jamb with a drawbar-slot remaining of the entrance on the west side. Earlier this century there were also traces of domestic ranges extending northwards and westwards from the tower to the outer wall, and of three small round towers projecting slightly from the outer wall. Lochore passed via an heiress to Sir Andrew Wardlaw of Torry. Their descendants lived here until Charles I's reign. In 1662 the estate went to John Malcome of Balbedie.

LOGIE   NO 408206

The 18th century and later mansion is said to incorporate an L-plan tower with blocked gun-loops built in the 16th centrury by the Wemyss family.

Lundin Tower

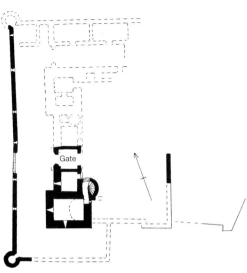

Plan of Macduff's Castle

LORDSCAIRNIE   NO 348178   V

This castle was probably built in the late 15th century by Alexander Lindsay, 4th Earl of Crawford, known as the Tiger Earl or Earl Beardie from his wild appearance in an age when beards were out of fashion. Of the later barmkin only a round tower with three gunloops which lay on the west side of the north-facing gateway now survives, but the shell of the three storey tower house is fairly intact, although the basement has lost its vault and the battlements have gone. It is 16.3m long by 10.1m wide over walls 1.7m thick and has corbelling for rounds on the south and west corners and a shallow wing at the north end of the NE wall containing the spiral staircase. The hall has a fine fireplace in the SW wall and several window embrasures, one of which retains seats. This chamber was used as a church by the minister of Moonzie for illicit services after he was ejected from his living by William III's government in 1689. The third storey was divided into a living room nearest the staircase and a bedroom beyond, each chamber having a fireplace, latrine and two windows. See page 10.

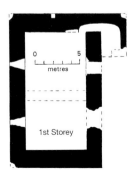

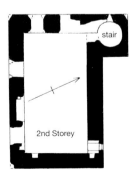

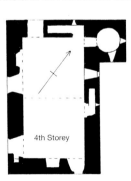

Plans of Lordscairnie Castle

LUNDIN   NO 399029

Of the late 16th century house of the Lundins of that Ilk only a turret containing a staircase and small upper rooms, plus a single storey 18th century outbuilding to the south survived demolition in 1876. The turret top with crenellated round turrets and a window with Y-tracery is late 18th century. The property passed by marriage to the Drummonds in 1670.

MACDUFF'S   NT 344972   F

This castle was the seat of the estate of East Wemyss and is named after the Thane of Fife of MacBeth's era who is said to have had a fortress here. Edward I of England stayed with Michael Wemyss, Macduff's descendant, in his castle here in 1304, but in 1306 Michael joined forces with Robert Bruce, and in consequence the Earl of Pembroke was ordered to destroy the castle and estate. In the 1340s the lands were split between heiresses but one portion eventually went to Sir John Wemyss of Kingaldrum and Rires, who is thought to have built a quadrangular court with a rectangular gatehouse in the NW corner. This building possibly incorporated late 13th or early 14th century work. Subsequently the family lived in nearby Wemyss Castle and Macduff's Castle passed to the Livingstones.

Robert Livingstone's daughter and her husband Sir James Hamilton of Finnart in 1530 exchanged East Wemyss for James Colville's barony of Ochiltree in Ayrshire. The Colvilles blocked up the gateway passage and remodelled the superstructure as a tower house. They then built a matching tower at the SW corner with a range containing a new gateway between the two towers. Regarded as dangerous, the upper parts of the NW tower were pulled down in 1967, burying the lower parts in a mound of debris. Apart from the west wall being missing above the vaulted basement the SW tower mostly survives. It had three upper rooms reached from the court by a spiral staircase in a round turret. In the late 16th century an outer court with an average width of about 9m was created around the north, west and SW sides. The west wall with a series of gunloops still remains. It has a small round turret at the SW corner and traces of another at the NW corner. There were buildings on the north side of this court. Little remains of ranges and screen walls facing the sea, except the bases of the SE corners of the original court and an outer east court at a lower level. In 1651 the Colvilles sold East Wemyss to John, lord Wemyss of Elcho, later Earl of Wemyss. The 2nd Earl preferred to reside at Wemyss Castle and Macduff's Castle was allowed to decay.

Lordscairnie Castle

Macduff's Castle

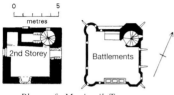

Plans of Monimail Tower

Menstrie Castle

MENSTRIE   NS 852968   V

Only the southern of two wings on the east side of the three storey main block of c1600 now survives. It was renovated to become the centre of a housing estate in the 1950s, and was divided into flats, except for one room reserved for meetings which has a set of panels with arms of baronets of Nova Scotia. At the SW corner is a round bartizan with one crossloop. In 1645 the castle, then belonging to the Earl of Stirling, was burnt by the Covenant army led by Argyll before his defeat by Montrose at Kilsyth. It was given to the Covenanter General Holborne in 1648, and in 1719 his descendants sold the castle to Alexander Abercromby of Tullibody.

MONIMAIL   NO 299141

The four storey 6m square tower which survives formed the NW corner of a quadrangular palace with three storey ranges on the west and north sides and lower ranges or screen walls on the other sides. The tower bears the date 1578 and the initials of Sir James Balfour of Pittendreich in a roundel at parapet level on the east side. Sir James had obtained this former palace of the archbishops of St Andrews from Archbishop Hamilton in 1564. He sold the house in 1592 to Sir Robert Melville of Murdocairnie, later Lord Melville, and also from 1627 onwards Lord Monimail. The parapet is carried on moulded corbel coursing and there is an octagonal caphouse with a damaged stone spire over the staircase in the NE corner. There are open bartizans at the other corners, that to the SE being polygonal. The basement was only reached by a hatch from above. Its location slightly below ground level made it suitable for later conversion into an ice-house.

Mountquhannie Castle

Monimail Tower

MOUNTQUHANNIE   NO 347212

On one side of the stable-court is a ruined early 16th century tower said to have still been habitable when the present house was built c1820. The staircase turret on the north side has gone but the rest stands high. It measures 13.2m long by 8m wide and has round corner bartizans. The basement has been subdivided later and there are many alterations to the three upper storeys. A tower dovecot stands at the SW corner of the court, which has the date 1683 over the gateway. The house has a reset stone with the date 1597 with the Balfour arms and initials. The property later passed to the Lumsdens and the Crawfords were owners at the time when the 1683 datestone was made.

MYRES   NO 242110

This castle is thought to have been built in the 1540s by John Scrymgeour, Macer to James V, and his Master of Works for building work at Holyrood and Linlithgow. It consists of a main block 9.6m long by 7.2m wide with a round tower at the SE corner, and a wing containing the entrance and staircase at the west end of the north side. A latrine turret is corbelled out from the NE corner at hall level. The basement contains two vaulted cellars in the main block and a room in the round tower furnished with oval gunloops at ground level. Above them is a second tier of rectangular gunloops once reached by wooden staging.

In 1611 James Scrymgeour sold Myres to the notary Stephen Paterson, Sheriff-Clerk of Fife. The only part not now ochre-harled is a square two storey upper part of grey ashlar then added on top of the round tower, the rooms being served by a stair in a spired turret in the western re-entrant angle. This part has a flat roof with a parapet embellished with garlands containing shields, the date 1616, and the initials and monogram of John Paterson and his wife Elizabeth Mure. In the mid 18th century Colonel George Moncrieff, a descendant of John Leslie, who purchased the estate in 1634, added a north wing and inserted a new southward facing entrance. The estate was sold again in 1820 to Professor John Bruce. He added the west wing in 1825 and carried out other alterations. Further work was carried out in the 1870s for Colonel Walter Hamilton Bruce, and a chapel was created out of a coachhouse of the 1820s for James Fairlie, a Roman Catholic who purchased Myres in 1887.

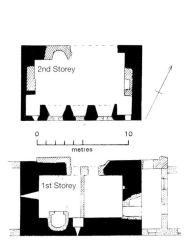

Plans of Mountquhannie Castle

Myres Castle

NAUGHTON   NO 373246

When James Morison built a new house here in 1793 he mostly dismantled a nearby 16th century tower lying at the SE end of a long court upon a sheer-sided rock approached from the west. Fragments of the courtyard walls remain, along with one side of the tower, parts of a nearby round tower, and traces of a long north range probably built by Peter Hay of Durie after he purchased Naughton in 1621. He is commemorated on a tablet now built into the east end of the range. The Hays had held Naughton at an earlier petiod, but it had passed by marriage to the Crichtons in 1513. In the court is a well now just 3m deep. The garden house at the west end has gablets of late medieval traceried window-heads, probably from Balmerino Abbey. Further west is a double dovecot with the dates 1636 and 1750, the latter with initials of James Morison.

NEWARK   NO 518012   V

In the 15th century the Kinloch family built here a palace or hall house 23.6m long by 8.5m wide with a court up to 16m in width between it and a cliff above the sea. The building contained a hall and private room end to end over three spacious vaulted cellars, although little now remains above the vaults. It passed to the Sandilands famly, who in the early 16th century added a narrow extension containing two upper rooms over a kitchen. On the NE corner is a drum tower 8m in diameter flanking the adjacent north facing gateway into the court, of which the the east jamb survives. Excavations in preparation for a possible restoration project have shown that the tower has two further storeys with gunports now buried in the infill of what must have once been a deep ditch protecting the vulnerable north side of the court. This ditch may have been a relic of an older fortress on this site.

It is first referred to as the "Newark of St Monans" in a charter of 1545, when lands belonging to the Prior of Pittenweem were transferred to Sir James Sandilands of Cruivie, and in 1645 another Sir James Sandilands, later Lord Abercrombie, was served heir to his grandfather of the lands "with the tower and fortalice of St Monance called the New-Werk". In 1649 the castle was sold to General Sir David Leslie. Between 1661, when Charles II created him Lord Newark, and his death in 1682 he remodelled the apartments, adding a further storey and the curvilinear Baroque-style gables of which only one fragment remains. There were outbuildings of this period and earlier in the court, and to the NW are remains of vaulted cellars against the cliff edge, so that they were mostly or entirely below courtyard level.

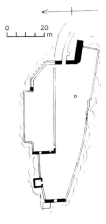

Newark Castle   *Naughton: plan*

Otterston Castle   *Newark Castle*

OTTERSTON   NT 165852

James Henderson, Lord Justice Clerk, acquired Otterston in the time of James IV, the barony being resigned and regranted in 1511. The house once dated 1589 (the lintel bearing that year was removed to Cockairnie) was much altered in 1851, and has now been demolished except for a round tower standing at the NE corner of the barmkin. The tower was given a crenellated parapet c1800, and has beside it the east jamb of the barmkin gateway. The main block was given two wings towards the court in the 17th century, that to the east having on it the date 1636 or 86.

PARBOATH   NO 322176

In a field 270m SW of the farm is a fragment of a vaulted cellar of a castle of the Setons.

PITCAIRLIE   NO 236148

Pitcairlie originally belonged to the Leslies of Lindores. Tte house began in the late 16th century as an L-plan building with a SW wing with the upper floors jettied out and surmounted by an ashlar parapet with shallow angle-rounds with long waterspouts. In c1730 the main block was lengthened westwards and widened into a double-pile but the two eastern bays of an intended seven bay north facade were never built. A large hip-roofed pavilion was added at the SW corner. It was then sold to the Cathcarts of Carbiston and further alterations were carried out in the early 19th century.

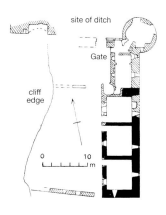

Plan of Newark Castle

Plan of Pitcullo Castle

Pitcruivie: plan

Pitcruive Castle

Randerston

PITCRUIVIE   NO 413046

This tower was built c1500 by Patrick, 4th Lord Lindsay of the Byres. His son Sir John was designated "of Pitcruivie" in 1511 and 1524. The tower measures 12m by 8m over walls 1.8m thick at the level of the barrel-vaulted hall. The round-arched entrance with a drawbar-slot is in the west wall at this level. Within this end, which was screened off with a gallery above, is a trapdoor in the vault of the cellar. A stair opened off the screens passage in a shallow wing, now ruined, projecting from the north wall. It seems that this was a later alteration and that a stair wing in the diagonally opposite corner existed or was intended. Its doorway to the hall has been blocked by remodelling which has included the hall vault and the fireplace at the east end. The window embrasures with seats on each side, however, are original.

PITCULLO   NO 413193

In the 1970s and 80s this ruined late 16th century building was re-roofed after being ruined for several generations, and it was restored to its original L-shape, a slightly later wing over-lapping the SE corner being removed. Because of the slope of the ground a sub-basement was provided at the east end, giving two cellars there, one above the other. The upper cellar now has an 18th century doorway to the outside, and a modern south window. A kitchen with a fireplace and oven in the west gable occupies the other half next to the wing. The wing contains a wide stair from the entrance (covered by one gunport) up to the hall and then a stair in a round turret with a square caphouse is corbelled out over the re-entrant angle. The length of the building, 15.2m, allows space for a private room east of the hall. Off the lobby between the two rooms opens a stair in a turret on the north side. This turret is an elongated round below and a rectangle above and facilitates access to the bedroom over the private room. This bedroom and that over the hall are partly within the roof, and have dormer win-dows. Pitcullo was held by the Sibbald family in the 15th century, but had passed to the Balfours by James IV's reign. It was later held by the Trents.

Pitcullo Castle

Pitfirrane Castle

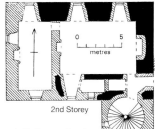

2nd Storey

Plan of Pitfirrane Castle

PITFIRRANE   NT 063861

In 1583 a three storey tower of c1500 was heightened by one storey and given a new ash-lar-faced west end containing an extra tier of chambers, the topmost having closets within round bartizans. At the same time a wing was added on the south side to contain a new entrance and a wide stair up to the third storey, above which access is by a turret stair corbelled out over the re-entrant angle. Over the entrance are the arms of the Halket family and James VI. Scars on the SE corner are relics of a demolished wing of c1680. The turret roofs are probably of the 1850s, when a round NE tower and a low servant's wing were added. The present owners, a golf club, have added a single storey extension on the south side. A 16th century yett from the entrance to a self-contained ground level room is fixed to a wall.

PITREAVIE   NT 117847

The ashlar-faced four storey house has two wings facing north, each of which has ornamental gunloops below the slit windows, and a doorway towards the court with initials on the pediments of Sir Henry Wardlaw, Chamberlain to James VI's consort Anne of Denmark. He acquired the estate in 1615 and built the house c1630, dying in 1638. His son was created a baronet of Nova Scotia in 1631. In the re-entrant angles are small round turrets supporting wide conical-roofed stair turrets corbelled out from a stringcourse. The house was sold in 1703 to Lord Rosebery, and again in 1711 to the Blackwood family. In a remodelling of 1885 by the Beveridge family it was given two south wings to make an H-plan, a dining room was added on the east, and the east wing given a balustraded porch. See page 16

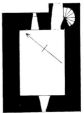

Pittarthie Castle

Pitteadie: plans

PITTARTHIE   NO 522091

This ruin was probably built in the 1580s for James Monypenny of Pitmellie. He originally held the lands from the Archbishop of St Andrews and in 1598 resigned them to Andrew Logan of Easter Granton. They were sold to the Bruce family in the 1630s, and over the south window of the hall is a segmental pediment dated 1682 with initials of William Bruce. A stair projection was then added near the east end of the north wall, giving access from a private room at that end of the hall (probably an original subdivision) to a bedroom at that end of the third storey. At the SW corner is a wing flanking both the west and south walls. It contains spacious living rooms over a kitchen with a big fireplace in the north wall. A staircase turret lies in the east re-entrant angle. There is a gunloop covering the roll-moulded entrance, and many of the windows have gunloops in their sills. The basement arrangements of the main block are somewhat obscured by rubble from fallen vaults. The SE corners of the wing and stair turret are rounded, and there is also a curve to the outer corner of the small projection lying in the west re-entrant angle. See page 11.

PITTEADIE   NT 257891

This tower measuring 11m by 8.2m over walls 1.6m thick was built in the late 15th century by the Vallance family. It later passed to the Sandilands family but in 1612 was declared to be the principal messuage of a barony created for John Boswell. A garden wall east of the tower has a round-arched gateway surmounted by a pediment with the date 1686 and initials of William Calderwood, apothecary and burgess of Edinburgh.

The tower has a wing projecting 1.2m from the east wall, just sufficient to accommodate a spiral staircase there. The entrance at the foot of this staircase is 17th century, and the original stair lay in the south wall beside the wing. At hall level this wall was thinned and given two new windows in the 17th century, when the room was probably subdivided, having an inserted fireplace in the west wall beside a mural chamber in addition to an original fireplace at the east end. The storey above was also subdivided with new fireplaces at each end, and the original east fireplace converted into a window embrasure. Opening off the attic above was a closet in a round bartizan on the SW corner, and a turret stair served two upper rooms over the main staircase in the wing.

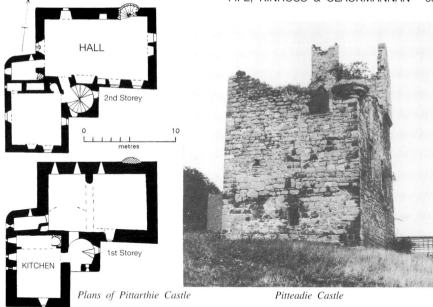

HALL

2nd Storey

0   10
⌊ ⌊ ⌊ ⌊ ⌊ ⌊ ⌋
metres

1st Storey

KITCHEN

Plans of Pittarthie Castle   *Pitteadie Castle*

PITTENCRIEFF   NT 087873   V

Sir Alexander Clerk's T-plan house of the 1630s, now lying in a public park just to the SW of the abbey of Dunfermline, was given a third full storey in 1731, the date on the SE skewputt. Robert Lorimer's remodelling of 1908-11 of the interior re-used one original lower ceiling.

PITTENWEEM   NO 549027   V

The 15th century gatehouse on the east site of the priory precinct has corbelling for a former machicolated parapet. The western range with a mid 16th century oriel was adapted as the manse in the 1580s. It is now a private residence called Great House.

PITTILLOCK   NO 278052

An L-plan 16th century tower of the Bruces is said to be incorporated in a mansion of c1850. It passed to the Lumsdens, then to the Baillies of Falkland, and then to the Balfours.

RANDERSTON   NO 608108

The castle mentioned in 1528 is thought to have stood by the shore 1km east of the present building, which is probably of c1580-1600. It has a main block 10m long by 7m wide with a SE wing boldly projecting from both the south and east walls. In the western re-entrant angle is a circular staircase turret with gunloops and the entrance. Higher up this turret is corbelled out into a square caphouse. Round bartizans on the NW corner of the main block and the SE corner of the wing have had their upper parts removed and the roofs swept down over them. The main block contains two vaulted cellars linked by a passage to the stair, a hall above, and an attic on top. The single storey block south of the wing is probably 19th century. Randerston was granted to Thomas de Myrtoun, Dean of Glasgow by James I in 1429 after being resigned by Sir John Sibbald of Balgonie. The estate remained with the Myrtouns or Mortons until sold in the early 17th century to a younger brother of Moncrieffe of Balcaskie. His heirs sold the house in 1663 to Michael Balfour of Pitmedden, a younger son of Balfour of Denmylne. See illustrations on pages 12 and 62.

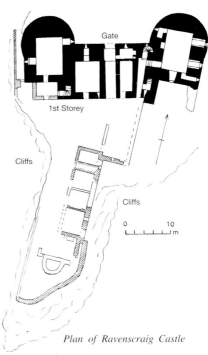

The east tower of Ravenscraig Castle

Plan of Ravenscraig Castle

RAVENSCRAIG   NT 291925   HS

Ravenscraig was begun in 1460 as a jointure house for James II's consort Mary of Gueldres. The castle was able to accommodate the Queen's steward and other servants for 25 days in 1461 but was left incomplete when she died in 1463. Further work, was, however carried out after it was granted in 1470 to William Sinclair, Earl of Caithness as part of an exchange in which the Crown took over the earldom of Orkney. The site is a narrow promontory jutting out into the Firth of Forth and rising 24m in a vertical cliff above the beach. The court lay below the level of the ground to the north, from which it was divided by a dry ditch and a range containing a passage flanked by guard-rooms. A hall may have been intended above, but there is now just a mid 16th century screen wall with two gunloops. There are U-shaped towers at each end of the range but the effect is far from symmetrical as the western tower of four storeys and an attic rises high above the court, whilst the east tower starts from a much lower level, and has just three storeys, so that its wall-walk and attic of c1600 are at the same level as the screen wall. Possibly this tower was intended to be two storeys higher. It has a well in its basement, clearly the reason why the builders bothered to raise a structure from so far below courtyard level. The two upper storeys contain pleasant rooms with latrines in the SE corner, fireplaces, and pairs of eastern window embrasures with seats.

The western tower is thought to have been built first, the ashlar being darker than the rest. The basement is entered directly from the court and has a gunloop covering the gateway. Only a hatch in the vault linked it with the upper levels, which are served by a spiral staircase in the SE corner, access to which is by an external forestair. The upper rooms have latrines in the SW corner and window embrasures with seats. The original wall-walk was replaced c1600 when the walls were covered with sloping slabs continuing the line of the attic roof, which was thus better protected from cannon-fire. Further south are remains of a later service range and walling designed to close off the already very difficult access up the side of the cliff from the beach. See illustrations on pages 8 and 10.

RIRES   NO 464046

Only a ditch now remains of this castle. A tower built in 1392 by Sir John Wemyss was be-sieged in 1402 by the Duke of Rothesay. It was completely demolished c1840.

ROSSEND   NT 230855   V

Overlooking Burnisland Harbour is a castle purchased and restored for their own use by a firm of architects in 1975. The east wing was built in the 1550s by Peter Dury, to whom the property had been transferred by his father George, Commendator of Dunfermline Abbey. On the east wall is a plaque with the arms of St Margaret founder of the abbey, and evidently contemporary with the stone now lying above the entrance of the modern north porch with the date XXII MAII 1554. This wing has four storeys, although the south end originally only had three. The 19th century top stage at that end is raised on corbelling originally for a parapet around a gun-platform commanding the harbour. Each storey was subdivided, the basement having a kitchen with a wide fireplace at the north end next to the staircase and entrance both set in a wing on the west side. The second storey rooms in later years formed a drawing room with a bedroom leading off to the south. This room is said to have been occupied by Queen Mary in 1563 and to have been the place where the poet Chastelard made amorous overtures to her. The block extending out from the middle of the west side is mostly late 16th century. It contains a long hall over three vaulted cellars linked by a passage along the north side. The south front of this wing has gunports covering the harbour and medieval lancets probably reset from a chapel on or near this site. There is a very modern-looking stair turret at the west end (not shown on the plan).

Rossend was held by Sir Robert Melville when he was forfeited in 1571, when it briefly returned to the David Dury before going back to the Melvilles. A remarkable ceiling of c1616 with initials of Sir Robert Melville of Burntisland was discovered in the drawing room in 1957 when vandals entered the then derelict building and cast a large stone down through the de-cayed floor of the room above. The ceiling was later removed to the Royal Museum of Scot-land in Edinburgh. In 1646 Sir James Melville refortified the position, and probably of that period are remains of two round bastions and a triangular one to the south. Two doorways on the north side, one dated 1665, are relics of alterations carried out by General James Wemyss, created Lord Burntisland in 1672. A garden wall to the west is dated 1713.

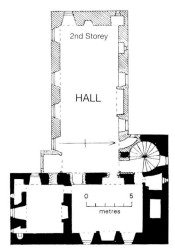

Plan of Rossend Castle   *Rossend Castle*

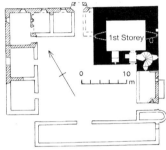

Rosyth Castle

Rosyth Castle: plan & section

ROSYTH   NT 110821

Within the secure compound of a dockyard are a 15th century tower and remains of two ranges out of four which were set around a court. Until the surrounding land was reclaimed the site was an island approached by a causeway from the north. Rosyth was made into a barony for Sir James Stewart in 1428 but the tower may be half a century later than that. It measures 14.2m by 12.4m over walls 2.8m thick and contained five storeys and an attic. There were vaults over the second storey retainers' room and the fourth storey room. The latter space was thrown into one with the hall below by removing its floor when large new mullion-and-transom windows were inserted in 1635. That date appears on one of the transoms along with initials of James Stewart and Margaret Napier. The hall fireplace is also probably of that period, but the segmental-arched buffet recess in the south wall is original. A service stair connects the hall with the room below. Both the parapet and the SE stair wing are of minimal projection. Tusking on the tower and the location of a doorway leading out from the staircase onto a former wall-walk suggest a 12m high range was added later, unless the barmkin wall in its original form was really that high. The north range of the court was added to an older western range. It contained a hall over the gateway passage and several cellars. There are gunloops in the outer wall and in the porch in front of the entrance, and there were bartizans on the corners. The initials M.R. for Maria Regina appear over the gateway with the Royal Arms and the date 1561. See page 9.

RUMGALLY   NO 407149

The house is said to incorporate an L-plan 16th century tower of the Scotts of Balwearie with a round stair turret within the re-entrant angle. In the 1650s it was acquired by James MacGill, minister of Largo. See page 70

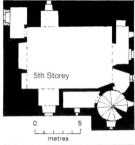

Rosyth Castle:
plans of tower

Gateway of St Andrews Castle

ST ANDREWS   NO 513169   HS

By the late 12th century the bishops of St Andrews had moved out of the precinct of the cathedral priory into a castle set on a low cliff not far to the north. Incorporated in the Fore Tower are some remains of a gatehouse probably built c1200 by Bishop Roger. In 1304 the castle was prepared for a visit by Edward I of England and Queen Margaret. It was dismantled by the Scots at some point afterwards but was repaired by Bishop William Lamberton c1315-20. The lowest part of the outer section of the Fore Tower is thought to be part of work executed in 1336 under the control of the English lords de Beaumont and de Ferrers on behalf of Edward III of England and his puppet King of Scots Edward Balliol. In 1337 the castle was captured and destroyed after a three week siege by Sir Andrew Moray.

The castle probably lay in ruins until restored by Bishop Walter Trail, who died within it in 1401. The superstructure of the Fore Tower, which then ceased to be a gateway, plus the existing curtain walls of the courtyard, together with the basements of the rectangular NE and NW towers are thought to be of his period. In the castle the young James I was educated by Bishop Wardlaw prior to the attempt to send the prince to France that led to his capture by the English. After Archbishop Alexander Stewart was killed at Flodden in 1513 Gavin Douglas occupied the castle, but was driven out by Prior John Hepburn, a rival contender for the vacant bishopric. In 1546 Cardinal David Beaton, Archbishop since 1539, was murdered in the castle by a party of Protestants who entered the building with workmen employed on strengthening the defences. A pair of circular blockhouses, of which little now survives, had been built at either end of the landward side and work was then proceeding on other buildings. With assistance sent by sea from England the Protestant party managed to hold out against a besieging force for an entire year until a French fleet broke the supply line. The castle was much damaged by cannon-fire during this siege, during which were dug the remarkable mine and countermine which still survive and can be inspected by visitors. The entrance to the third countermine that eventually proved successful lies outside the walls, other attempts from within the walls having failed, and this suggests there were then earth or timber outer lines of defence which have left no traces, although the ditch in front of the walls still remains, and may go back to the late 12th centuy.

St Andrews Castle: Fore Tower

Rumgally

The next archbishop was John Hamilton (1549-71) whose badge of a five-pointed star appears on a panel on the Fore-Tower and over the gateway, evidence of the rebuilding then needed to make the place habitable again. In 1587 the Act of Annexation transferred the castle and other church property to the Crown, and in 1608 James VI granted the castle to the Earl of Dunbar, although it reverted to the archbishopric later. It then fell into ruin and in 1654 was partly dismantled to provide materials for repairing harbour walls.

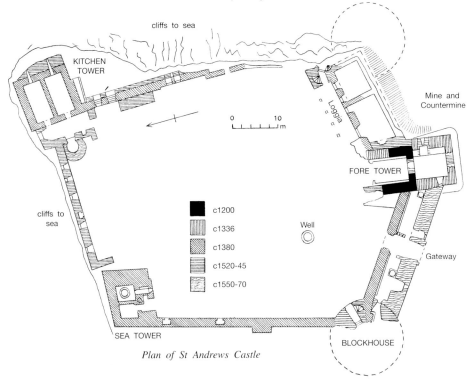

Plan of St Andrews Castle

St Andrews Castle

The lower parts of curtain walls about 2m thick enclose a pentagonal court about 60m across. The wall on the east side is not an outer curtain but the thinner inner wall of a range containing the hall and other apartments, the rest of which has fallen into the sea, along with all of the eastern blockhouse. Only the two vaulted cellars remain of the Kitchen Tower in the NE corner. The kitchen itself lay above at the level of the hall, with at least one private chamber above. The east wall of the tower has 16th century buttressing. To the west was a passage, probably from a seagate or postern. Beyond lay the north range, with a brewhouse or other service rooms on the lowest level. The Sea Tower also contains two cellars but they are smaller than those of the other tower owing to the greater thickness of the walls. The east cellar contains a round opening into a bottle-shaped pit-prison 7m deep carved in the native rock. The much ruined upper storey was rebuilt later, probably after being destroyed by cannon-fire from French ships during the siege of 1546-7. The outer part of the 16m diameter west blockhouse has been destroyed but the inner parts remain, with a gunport flanking the nearby gateway and the lower part of a staircase to the upper storey.

Slezer's print of 1718 shows that the upper stage of the south range had on either side of the ornate central gateway a symmetrical arrangement of windows for the second and third storeys. This range was created in the 1550s by building a new outer wall in front of the old one. Its base may in fact predate the 1546-7 siege, since the vaulted lowest level contains two trial countermine entrances. The uppermost level perhaps formed a long gallery, a rarity in Scotland, but common enough in late 16th century England. Early 16th century chequered corbelling and a crow-stepped gable for an attic within the destroyed parapet crown the outer part of the Fore Tower. It had four storeys below the battlements in the eventual layout, which has different floor levels from the original 13th and 14th century work. Part of the outer gate of 1336 is visible, with one of the old drawbridge chases high above it. On the east side is a gunport inserted into a former postern. The older, northern part of the tower is much more ruined. A vault was later inserted into it at ground level. Adjoining the east side of the Fore Tower are the very ruined lower parts of a range which contained a chapel with two-light traceried windows on the upper floor. A loggia was built against the northern side of this range in the 16th century. A well lies in the centre of the courtyard.

St Andrews: Cathedral-priory precinct wall

The precinct of the cathedral-priory was walled by the late 14th century and the main gateway facing NW is of that period, but most of the existing wall was built in the early 16th century under priors John and Patrick Hepburn. The circuit is almost complete and of sixteen towers recorded in 1683 thirteen still survive. Two are rectangular and the others are slender rounds with image-niches, keyhole-shaped gunloops and corbelled parapets. The cathedral itself formed part of the circuit and one gate adjoins its NE corner. Other gates are the Mill Port or Sea Yett, and the Tiends Gate in Abbey Walk which gave access to a barn.

The town of St Andrews never had serious defences but it presumably had a palisade and ditch throughout the later medieval period. Across South Street is the West Port, the town's main gateway, built in 1589 and modelled on the Netherbow Port at Edinburgh. It has a round-arched opening flanked by semi-octagonal towers with gunloops and corbelled parapets with cannon-spouts, a symbol of civic pride more than a real fortification.

St Andrews: West Port

Fireplace in Sauchie Tower

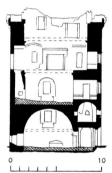

Sauchie: entrance doorway

SAUCHIE   NS 896957   V

This fine ashlar-faced tower is thought to have been built by Sir James Shaw in the 1430s after his marriage to Mary Annan, heiress of the estate. It measures 11.6m by 10.4m and has the west wall substantially thicker than the rest to contain the round-arched entrance, the staircase and mural chambers on the second and third storey levels. A hall with a fine fireplace lies at third storey level over a cellar and a vaulted retainers' loft, and the laird's bedroom with seats in three window embrasures and a latrine and fireplace lay above. Within the roof (recently restored) lay a windowless fifth storey and an attic within a parapet upon corbelling with small angle-rounds, whilst there is a hexagonal caphouse over the staircase. Part of the barmkin wall survives and projecting from it is a truncated stair-turret with loops with top and bottom roundels. It formed part of a 17th century range demolished c1920. The property passed to the Cathcarts in 1752. See picture on back of cover.

4th Storey

2nd Storey

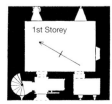

1st Storey

Sauchie: plans & section

Sauchie Tower

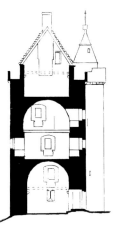

Scotstarvit: plans & section

SCOTSTARVIT   NO 370113

The Inglis family of Tarvit are thought to have built this fine ashlar-faced tower c1500. It measures 10.2m by 8.2m and rises 16m to a wall-walk with a parapet on double-member corbels. There are vaults over the second and fourth of six levels. A staircase in a shallow SE wing rises from the adjacent entrance through the full height of the building and ends in a spired caphouse. The hall at third storey level has a fireplace in the west wall and a latrine near the NE corner. Beside the stair at this level is a tiny chamber with a window and sink between it and the hall. The fourth storey was probably subdivided, one of the rooms having a small north fireplace. The fifth storey has a west fireplace. The existing attic was built as a study for Sir John Scot, who purchased and renamed the estate in 1611. Within this study he wrote his celebrated satirical book "Scot of Scotstarvit's Staggering State of Scots Statesmen". A chimneypiece from this room has been removed to Hill of Tarvit but there remain over the stair-head doorway a panel with the date 1617 and arms and initials of Sir John and his wife Dame Anne Drummond.

Two views of Scotstarvit Tower

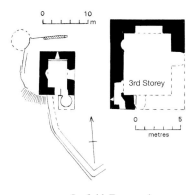

0   10
m

3rd Storey

0   5
metres

Seafield Tower: plans

Seafield Tower

SEAFIELD   NT 280885   F

This tower on a rock where a burn meets the sea was built c1500 by the Moultray family. It passed to the Earl of Melville after the last Moultray was killed in the 1715 Jacobite rebellion. The tower measures 9.2m by 7.7m and contained a cellar and sleeping loft under a vault, a hall above, and two upper storeys. It was originally entered at ground level in the south end wall beside a shallow staircase wing, but in the late 16th century the wing was rebuilt larger, blocking part of the doorway and necessitating making another on the east side. The hall has a wide fireplace in the north wall, a latrine in the SW corner and one jamb of a large east window. The fourth storey has a fireplace in the west wall. Extending south from the tower are the lower parts of a wall 1.2m thick closing off the west side of a courtyard towards the sea. The thinner walls north and west of the tower with traces of a former round tower on the corner late late 16th century. A plan of 1774 suggests there was another court on the north.

STRATHENDRY   NO 226020

Over the entrance to this T-plan house of c1600 are arms and initials of Thomas Forrester and Isobel Learmonth. The Forresters had inherited the lands from the Strathendries in 1496. The east gable has a corbelled parapet, more of a gallery for taking the air than for defence. The stair turret projecting 4m from a main block 11.7m long by 7.8m wide seems to have been rebuilt by Sir Edward Douglas in 1699, his initials and that year appearing over its west doorway. The ogival roof on the turret dates only from 1906. The court to the south and east may correspond to a former barmkin, but the outbuildings are all of 1824, 1845, and 1943.

STRATHMIGLO   NO 220104

Nothing now stands of a castle east of the village. It was demolished in 1734 for materials to build a steeple in front of the town hall. An armorial panel upon this tower is said to be a relic of the castle. A fortalice is mentioned in a charter of lands granted to Sir William Scot in 1509. James V nicknamed the building "Cairnie Flappet" from a poorly constructed addition put up in a rather a hurry by the Scotts of Balwearie to accommodate him here. The estate passed c1600 to the Balfours of Burleigh, and then later to the Skenes of Hallyards.

STRATHVITHIE   NO 531118 (approx)

The Lumsdens had a moated castle here which was held in the 16th century by Lady Margaret Erskine, firstly mistress of James V and then much later on jailor of Queen Mary. The estate passed to her bastard son Lord James Stewart, Regent Moray, shot and killed at Linlithgow in 1570. The building was still complete in 1710 but nothing of it now remains.

Tullibole Castle

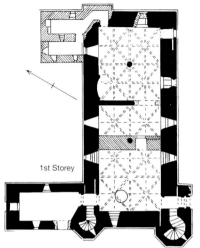

1st Storey

Plan of Tulliallan Castle

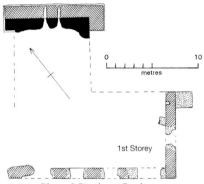

0   10
metres

1st Storey

Plan of Struthers Castle

STRUTHERS   NO 377097

In 1392 Sir William Lindsay of The Byres obtained Struthers and Wester Markinch from his father-in-law Sir William Keith in exchange for the castle and barony of Dunnottar. Struthers became the chief seat of the Lindsays of The Byres, who later succeeded to the earldom of Crawford. Charles II stayed for two days at the castle in 1651, and it was occupied by Cromwellian forces in 1653. Fragments remain of an L-shaped 16th century house with big 18th century windows facing SW, plus a cellar and buttress further east. A massive gable to the NE has heavy side buttresses carrying corbelling for round bartizans at fourth storey level. This gable incorporates an earlier thin end wall of uncertain date.

Struthers Castle

Tulliallan Castle

TULLIALLAN   N S 927888

This emigmatic ruin lies hidden in woods near where there was once an important ferry over the Forth. The ditch around a D-shaped enclosure must have existed by 1304 when Edward I ordered the walls (probably meaning palisades) to be strengthened. On a rock outcrop at the NE side of the enclosure stands an ashlar-faced block of the type usually known in Scotland as a palace. Such buildings usually contained dark cellars under a hall and chamber set end-to-end. Here, however, the lower rooms have very high quality quadripartite rib-vaults with a row of central octagonal piers. Since the eastern lower room has a fine fireplace and once had a large trefoil-headed window high up on the north side it must have been a living room or an office or courtroom. Only after a blocking wall and other alterations were inserted in the 16th century was the lower storey used for storage. The east room has an entrance from the outside at the east end of the south wall. There is a doorway at the NW corner (also with a drawbar slot and facing towards a small wing), but the main entrance, furnished with a portcullis groove, lies in a shallow projection at the SW corner. It was probably approached over the ditch by a timber bridge with a lifting middle section. The hall above has a fireplace on the north side and large windows facing south. There are staircases in polygonal turrets on both of the western corners, that beside the main entrance being the principal stair, and the other one serving a small upper chamber in a narrow NW wing. In the 15th century a narrow NE wing was added to contain a prison reached by a hatch through the floor of a room above. In 1619 five men were accused of starving another man to death in this prison. This wing was doubled in width and given a third storey and caphouse in the 16th century, when the west end of the main block was given a third storey. The 14th century work is attributable to the Douglas family, who granted the fortalice and lands of Tulliallan to Sir John Edmonstone of that Ilk in 1402. It passed to the Blackadders by marriage in 1486. Sir John Blackadder was executed in 1531 for killing the Abbot of Culross, whilst Patrick Blackadder lost his lands in the Border, and probably also his life, to the Homes. The castle was acquired by the Bruces of Carnock in 1605 and was inhabited until the 1660s.

TULLIBOLE   NO 053006

John Halliday purchased this estate in 1598. He was dead by 1607 and the present T-plan house with conical-roofed bartizans on the staircase turret bears the date 1608 and initials of his son John and Helen Oliphant. The entrance into the foot of the wing is defended by a machicolation high above. The west end of the main block 19.4m long by 8m wide containing a private room leading off the hall may have once been an earlier self-contained tower, this end being slightly higher than the rest. The kitchen lies at the other end, next to the entrance. The cellar in the middle has a stair in a projecting turret linking it with the private room, and the west end of the hall, and the bedrooms above, but it also has a separate service stair up to where a wide service area was screened off at the west end of the hall. In a later remodelling this service area was given three large new windows. A castle at Tullibole is recorded as early as 1304. It passed by marriage to Archibald Moncrieff in 1722.

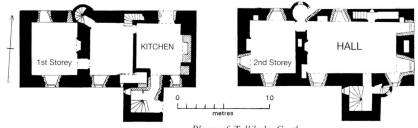

Plans of Tullibole Castle

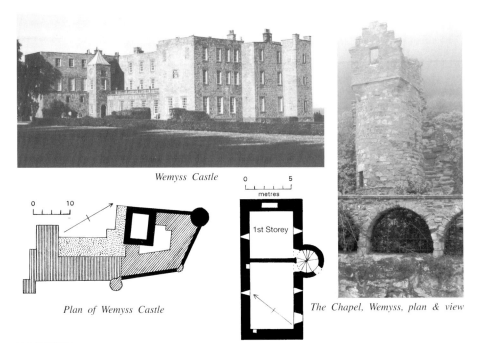

Wemyss Castle

Plan of Wemyss Castle

1st Storey

The Chapel, Wemyss, plan & view

WEMYSS   NT 329951   V

It was probably the Sir John Wemyss who lived from 1430 to 1502 who built the tower house forming the core of this mansion, although the 16th century panel over the gateway has had the date 1421 added in the margin, which would relate to the time of his grandfather and namesake, who died in 1428. The tower has a spiral staircase in the NE corner and contained a vaulted cellar and a hall over, above which it was entirely rebuilt c1600. The round tower at the north corner of the court to the north and east, and parts of the curtain walling set on a cliff edge may be contemporary with the main tower. Gradually the court was mostly filled with ranges to the east (where the hall lay), the north, and NW, leaving only a tiny central space. A boldly projecting round tower was added to the SE corner. There was a general heightening and remodelling with new moulded parapets all round later on, probably by the Sir John Wemyss who died in 1622. His son, another John, was created Lord Wemyss of Elcho in 1628, and Earl of Wemyss in 1633. David, 2nd Earl in the 1670s built a new L-shaped mansion to the south with a boldly projecting square wing at the SE corner. This effectively created an outer court with an open west side, but most of the space between the south wing and old tower forming the north wing was filled by a wide new range in 1874-6. This was removed in the 1930s and replaced by a single storey range with a three storey belltower beside the junction with the old tower house. The building now looks rather bleak, with flat roofs without gables, dormers, turrets or anything to relieve the horizontal effect at the top.

WEMYSS, THE CHAPEL   NT 319946

This four storey ruin of c1600 set only a little above above sea-level consists of a main block 15m long divided into two rooms at each level. Adjoining the crosswall is a round stair turret with a square caphouse. The lowest level is below ground level and contains a kitchen at the east end. The second storey rooms at ground level were storage spaces with only tiny loops for light. An oriel window opens out of the west end at third storey level.

OTHER FORMER CASTLES IN FIFE, KINROSS, & CLACKMANNAN

CAMBO NO 604115 House rebuilt after 1878 fire lies on site of castle of Morton family
CLATTO NO 358073 House mostly of 1845-50 on or near site of castle of Learmonths.
COCKAIRNIE NT 169853 Three storey house may incorporate 16th century work.
DALGETY NT 169838 No remains of favourite house of Chancellor Alexander Seton.
GARVOCK NT 105875 Seat of Wellwood family. Wall and tower still remained in 1785.
HALHILL NO 292132 Site of 16th century tower of the Melville family.
HARTSHAW NS 958915 Datestone of 1574 is the only relic of a castle of the Stewarts.
HILLSIDE NT 191856 Last remains, including 16th century dovecot, demolished in 1960.
INCHMURTACH NO 565132 Site of palace of William Lamberton, Bishop of St Andrews.
KINALDY NO 513104 Site of castle of Aytons, owners from 1539 until the 18th century.
KINCASK NO 541145 Site of Grundistouns' castle. Later passed to earls of Crawford.
KINCRAIG NO 466003 Site of castle of Gourlays of Kincraig, owners from 13th century.
KINNAIRD NO 273174 Site of house of Balfour family on former monastic lands.
LUTHRIE NO 332196 Site of castle or house of the Murray family.
MAIDEN NO 349015 Fine motte with summit 22m across. Traces of outer ditches, etc.
NEWHALL NO 598100 Site of castle of the Meldrum family.
PITLESSIE NO 336096 Site of castle of the Hamiltons of Bynnie
PITLOCHIE NO 175095 The Lundies of Balgonie had a "tower and fortalice" here in 1557.
PITLOUR NO 209113 Mansion of 1783 on or near site of a castle of the Scott family.
RANKEILOUR NO 330119 House on site of castle of Sibbald family, mentioned in 1540.
RATHILLET NO 359208 House of 1790. A Halkerstone seat until c1772. A 13th century
     document refers to the repair of the hall of the manor.
REEDIE NO 234107 Moncreiffes had a castle or house here before moving to Myres.
SALINE NT 025925 Site of palace of bishops of Dunkeld known as Kirklands.
SCOTSCRAIG NO 445283 Dalcleish mansion of 1817 near site of Scotts' castle.
TORRIE NT 015867 House on site of a castle of the Wardlaws of Torrie.

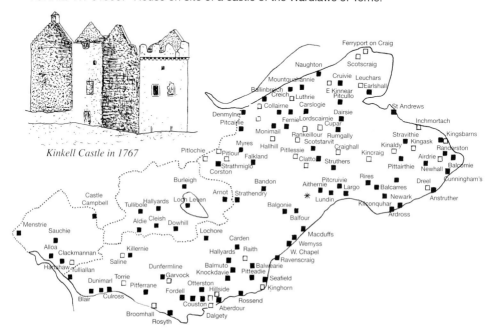

Kinkell Castle in 1767

CASTLES OF PERTHSHIRE

ABERUCHILL   NN 744212

In 1596 James VI gave Aberuchill to Colin, 2nd son of Campbell of Lawers, and the white-washed tower house with round bartizans and a round staircase turret was built soon after-wards, being dated 1607. It has a main block of three storeys and an attic measuring 12m by 6.3m and a wing 7m wide projecting 5.4m. Sir Colin Campbell of Aberuchill and Kilbryde was created a baronet in 1667 by Charles II, under whom he served as Lord Justice Clerk. He claimed over £17,000 worth of damage was done to his estates by the Jacobites under Dun-dee, and was granted compensation by an Act of Parliament, although he never received the money and in addition had to pay blackmail to Rob Roy MacGregor for protection. A large modern mansion now surrounds the tower.

AIRNTULLY   NO 091362

The farm called Stewart Tower lies on the site of a castle built by a branch of the Stewarts descended from the youngest illegitimate son of Robert II. In 1560 Regent Moray ordered Sir John Stewart of Airntully to strip Dunkeld Cathedral of images. The estate was later owned by the Steuart-Fotheringhams of Murthly.

ARDBLAIR   NO 164446   V

This is a whitewashed building with low two storey ranges set around three sides of a court with a screen wall and gateway facing the road. At one corner is a low tower of c1600 of three storeys and an attic with a wing overlapping two sides. There are two cellars in the main block. The wing contains the ornate entrance and main stair to the hall and then has bedrooms higher up, a left-hand turning stair being corbelled out over the angle towards the field. There is one gunloop on that side. Thomas Blair of Balthayock was granted the estate by Robert III in 1399. Patrick Blair of Ardblair was executed for his part in the murder of George Drummond of Ledcrieff in 1554, and others of this family were noted for their law-lessness. Over the courtyard gate are the year 1688 and the arms of the Oliphants of Gask, still owners in the 20th century. However it seems that Ardblair did not actually pass to that family of noted Jacobites until 1792.

ARNHALL   NS 764986

On the Keir estate are ruins of an L-planned building probably of early to mid 17th century date since it has large openings at ground level, and was quite low, the third storey being partly in the roof. There were round bartizans on the main block SE corner and the wing NW corner. The main block measures 11.7m by 6.4m and the wing is 5.3m wide and projects 5m. The lowest room in the wing was the only part to be vaulted.

Aberuchill Castle

Ashintully Castle

Ardblair

Ardblair

Plan of Ashintully Castle

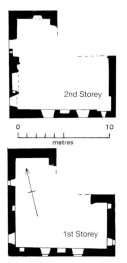

2nd Storey

0   10
|__|__|__|__|__|__|
       metres

1st Storey

Plans of Arnhall

ASHINTULLY   NO 101613

A framed panel on the door lintel is dated 1583 with the inscription "The Lord Defend This Hous" and the walls contain a number of gunports and shotholes. They presumably saw use in 1587 when the castle was besieged by a party of thirty Stewarts and Blairs later outlawed for their rough treatment of the laird of Ashintully, Andro Spalding. His initials and those of his wife, one of the Wemyss family, also appear on the panel. In 1677 the estate was erected into a barony for a later Andro Spalding. In was acquired by the Rutherfords in 1750. The four storey wing of the L-plan has an open wall-walk and parapet above the entrance. The three storey main block 11.3m long by 6.6m wide has been much modernised and extended. It had a cellar next to the entrance and a kitchen beyond, the vault of which has been removed. The stair lies not in the re-entrant angle next to the entrance, but in that on the opposite side, i.e. in the west end wall of the main block.

Arnhall

AUCHTERADER   NN 936134

In the steading of Castleton Farm is a fragment of walling. Two 16th century gunloops from it have been reset in more recent walling to the east. There are also traces of a moat in the garden to the south. Malcolm Canmore is said to have had a hunting seat here, and Edward I of England stayed for a while during one of his invasions. Here in the 1550s was signed a treaty between James V's widow Mary of Guise in her capacity as Regent and the Protestant Lords which granted freedom of worship within Scotland.

BALEDGARNO   NO 276304

The Castle Hill above the village is said to be the site of a castle built in 1101 by King Edgar, from whose name is derived the place name of Baledgarno. There are no visible remains.

BALHOUSIE   NO 116244   OP

A seat of the Earls of Kinnoull overlooking the North Inch north of the town centre of Perth has been encased in work of the 1860s. Prior to then a barmkin gateway survived. The Hay arms appear on one wall and a skewputt is dated 1631. The main block basement has two cellars and a kitchen without the usual connecting passage. The wing contains a wide stair from the entrance to the hall. A stair to a third storey and attic in the main block and two upper storeys in the wing is then corbelled out of the end wall. It has a square caphouse. The castle now houses the Black Watch Regimental Museum.

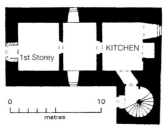

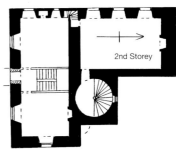

Plan of Balhousie Castle

Plan of Balmanno Castle

Balhousie Castle

Balmanno Castle

BALLOCH   NO 263498

A ruined castle here is indicated on Stobie's map of 1783. The only remains now are some dressed stones incorporated in the farmsteading. It was a seat of the Rollo family.

BALMANNO   NO 144156

The surrounding wet moat, now filled in on the east, goes back to the time of the Balmannos of that Ilk. The lofty whitewashed L-plan tower was built c1575 for George Auchinleck after his purchase of the estate. It passed in the late 17th century to the Murrays of Glendoick, and in 1752 went by marriage to the Belshes of Invermay. The original entrance lies at the base of a 21m high six storey square tower set between the wing and the main block. On one side of the tower is a round staircase turret which was heightened and given an ogival-shaped cap when Sir Robert Lorimer restored the building c1900. The present entrance lies at hall level in the main block opposite wall.

BALTHAYOCK   NO 175230

On the north edge of a ravine near a later mansion lies the Blairs' derelict 15th century tower. The reset heraldic panel dated 1578 with the initials M.B. and G.M. came from a demolished later extension. The tower measures 16.2m by 11.6m over walling 3.5m thick and has vaults over both the cellar and hall with just one more storey above. The upper openings are modernised and there are modern battlements and a flat roof. A basement loop has been broken open to make a lower entrance. External stairs rise over it up to the original entrance into the east end of the vaulted hall. From it a passage leads to a spiral stair leading up within the middle of the south wall, beside which is the head of a straight stair up from the vaulted cellar. The hall has a fireplace at the far end with loops set high up on either side of it. Close to this end each long wall contains a window embrasure with seats, off one of which leads a square mural room.

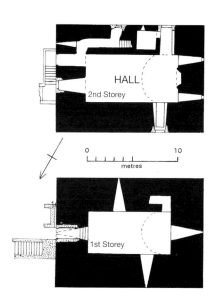

Plans of Balthayock Castle

Balthayock Castle

Balvaird Castle

Balvaird Castle

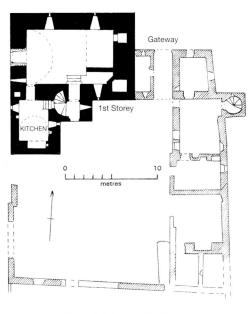

Plan of Balvaird Castle

BALVAIRD   NO 169118   HS

This fine L-plan tower house is thought to have been built by Sir Andrew Murray after he married the heiress Margaret Barclay. Their arms and the date 1567 once appeared over the gateway of the later court to the south and east of the tower. The main block measures 13.6m long by 9.1m wide and the wing is 5.6m wide and projects 5.4m. The staircase and entrance lie in a square turret set within the re-entrant angle. A kitchen lies in the base of the wing. The hall has a fine aumbry and fireplace and the window embrasures are fitted with seats and have access to mural rooms. The third storey contained a suite of two rooms for the laird, and there were two more rooms on the fourth storey, plus lesser rooms at these levels in the wing. The latrines were flushed by rainwater diverted from the wall-walk. The latrine-shaft has a removeable stone at the bottom. The corbelled parapet with angle-rounds is copied in miniature on a tiny top turret over the staircase. The building was re-roofed in the 1990s to preserve its fine features. The courtyard had ranges of offices and apartments on all four sides but most of them are reduced to fragments and foundations. However, the corbelled out storey containing a chapel over the gateway on the north remains fairly intact. In 1631 the Reverend Andrew Murray succeeded to Balvaird and in 1641 he was created Lord Balvaird by Charles I, an act calculated to annoy the Covenants, with whom Murray was unpopular. This title has passed down to the Murray earls of Mansfield.

BAMFF   NO 222515

In the SW corner of the house of 1828 and 1844 is a 16th century tower house rising four storeys above a vaulted basement with gunloops and originally also a well. The staircase was probably in the east corner with the entrance next to it. The Ramsays have had their seat here since at least the 1230s when Neis de Ramsay was physician to Alexander II. Alexander Ramsey served as physician to James VI and Charles I, and in 1666 Gilbert Ramsay was created a baronet by Charles II after the battle of Rullion Green.

BELMONT   NO 287439

The present castellated mansion, now a Church of Scotland Eventide Home, incorporates a small rectangular tower called Kirklands built in the 16th century by one of the bishops of Dunkeld. It passed to the Nairnes in the 1560s, and later was held by Sir George Mackenzie of Rosehaugh, a noted persecutor of the Covenanters. It later passed to the Wharncliffes and the Campbell-Bannermans. The tower has an ornamental quatrefoil-shaped gunloop at third storey level.

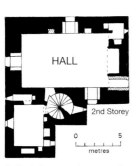

Balvaird: second storey plan

Belmont, formerly Kirklands

Blair Castle

BLACKCRAIG   NO 108534

Incorporated into the back of a mansion of 1856 is a three storey tower probably built by the Maxwells in the late 16th century. It has a round staircase turret with a square caphouse on the NW. The balcony on the main block is modern.

BLAIR   NN 866662   OP

In 1269 David, Earl of Atholl complained to Alexander III that while he had been away in England John Comyn or Cumming of Badenoch had invaded the district of Atholl and had commenced building a castle at Blair. The lower two storeys of the tower named after him measuring about 18m by 11m may perhaps go back to that period. What subsequently happened to this castle is not known, but Edward III of England is said to have stayed at Blair in 1336. The original earldom was forfeited for opposition to Robert Bruce, but in 1457 James II created the title anew for his maternal half-brother Sir John Stewart of Balvenie. The 3rd Earl is said to have built the second tower to the west and the hall block connecting them, but all these structures have been much altered since. The male line failed in 1595 and the earldom went to descendants of a brother of the 1st Earl, and in 1629 it was granted to John Murray, Master of Tullibardine, whose mother was heiress of the 5th Earl. In 1652 Blair Castle was captured and occupied by Cromwellian troops. The skeletons of three men found under the floor of the lowest room in the west tower in 1869 were thought to have been killed during the young Earl of Atholl's attempt to recapture the castle for the Royalist cause in 1654.

After the restoration of Charles II the then earl was created a marquess and his son John was created Duke of Atholl by Queen Anne in 1703. The 2nd Duke was in the middle of modernising the castle and laying out a new park when the Jacobite rebellion of 1745 broke out. The castle was visited by Prince Charles Edward but subsequently held Hanovarian troops and was besieged by a Jacobite force led by Lord George Murray, younger brother of the Duke. It was about this time that the old hall was converted into a Baroque dining room with a stucco ceiling and a splendid marble chimney-piece made in London in 1751. The castellated features subsequently removed were only restored by the 7th Duke in 1869. A block containing a new entrance hall was then added on the south side.

BRACO   NO 823113

The nucleus of the mansion is a four storey 16th century L-plan tower in the NW corner. Its wing no longer contains a staircase. The entrance is in the north wall. William Graham, 2nd son of the 3rd Earl of Montrose filled the re-entrant angle on the west side with an extension about the time of his being made a baronet in 1625. The castle was garrisoned by Jacobites in 1716 but abandoned after the battle of Sheriffmuir. A large extension with two wings on the east side was built by an 18th century laird who was equerry to George III, and who hoped in vain to entertain his master at Braco. General David Graham, who died in the 1790s, was the last of his family to live here. A low 19th century extension lies between the two Georgian wings.

BRAES OF TAYMOUTH   NN 791456

This is a three storey tower house c1600, still occupied and somewhat altered.

CALLANDER   NN 629076 & 629078

Reset upon the manse on the south bank of the river is a stone from the castle which lay upon this flat site, probably protected by marshes and a moat. The stone has the date 1596 and initials of Alexander Livingstone, 1st Earl of Linlithgow and his wife Elizabeth Hay, daughter of the 9th Earl of Erroll. Alexander was a favourite of James VI, and, after the King went to England in 1603, had custody here of the young Princess Elizabeth, later to become Queen of Bohemia. A fragment of masonry also survives in the garden. A motte 4m high and 12m by 7.5m across on top lies by the cemetery across the river.

CARDNEY   NO 050453

The present house here, latterly held by the MacGregors, is not ancient, but this was long a seat of a branch of the Stewerts descended from Robert, youngest illegitimate son of Robert II by Marion de Cardney of that Ilk. Her brother Robert was Bishop of Dunkeld and later a hostage for James I's ransom. Stewarts of Aintully, Dulaise and Murthly stem from this line.

CARDROSS   NS 605976

This house, a seat of the Erskine earls of Mar until the 20th century, comprises a five storey 16th century tower house with a slightly later three storey range added to it. Each part has a conical-roofed circular bartizan. Window lintels on the later part have initials of David Erskine and Margaret Murray and the date 1598, and John Erskine and his wife with the date 1747. The north front is 18th century and there is a modern range to the west.

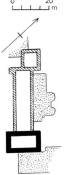

0   20
m

Blair: plan   *Cardross*

Carnbane Castle

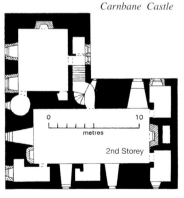

Carnbane Castle

CARNBANE   NN 677480

On a tree-clad bluff high above the road are ruins of a castle built in 1564 by Red Duncan Campbell The Hospitable. A block 15.4m long by 7.5m wide facing the approach and an isolating ditch 7m wide, contained rooms with gunports on either side of a gateway passage to a small court now only enclosed by buried foundations of its walls. It seems that there was another range of similar size filling the south end of the court. The gateway range contained an upper hall with a closet in the NW corner. The rooms below are choked with rubble from collapsed vaults, but one had a fireplace. A spiral stair in a square turret at the SW corner served the upper rooms.

Plan of Castle Huntly

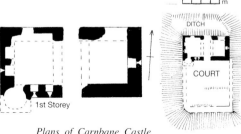

Plans of Carnbane Castle

Castle Huntly

CASTLE HUNTLY   NO 301292   V

Andrew, Lord Grey of Foulis is said to have been licensed by James II in 1452 to build this large and lofty L-plan tower with a a wing projecting from the west wall of a main block 19m long by 11.7m wide over walls 3.2m thick. There are numerous mural chambers, and a pit prison reached by a hatch in the lowest room of the wing has been sunk into the rocky bluff from which the building dominates the Carse of Gowrie. The entrance into the wing lay above the ground until the land level was raised later. A stair lies beside it in the re-entrant angle, and there is another stair in the south wall connecting the third and fourth storeys. The attic and present battlements are of c1800 when George Patterson remodelled the building and added wings on the north side. In the reign of James VI the Master of Grey was said to be the handsomest and wickedest man in Europe. In 1614 his son sold Castle Huntly to Patrick Lyon, 11th Lord Glamis, later created Earl of Strathmore and Kinghorne. He built the outer gateways and laid out the grounds with statues. The castle now serves as a borstal.

Castle   Menzies

CASTLE MENZIES   NN 837496   OP

The Menzies family had a group of estates around Weem from the 14th century. Their chief seat at Comrie was burned in 1488 and Sir Robert Manzies then built a new house called the Place of Weem near the site of the present building. In 1502 this castle was in turn wrecked by Neil Stewart of Garth. The older castle is specifically referred to in a document of 1572 also mentioning the existing castle, which is essentially of 1571-77. The former year appears on a panel over the original entrance with impaled arms and initials of James Menzies and Barbara Stewart, daughter of the Earl of Atholl, and the later date appears on the pediment of a dormer window of the fourth storey. The castle was occupied by General Monk's forces in 1646 and was captured and occupied by the Jacobites in 1715. Prince Charles Edward stayed for two nights in 1746, but four days later the family were ejected and the castle occupied by the Duke of Cumberland's forces. Egidia, last of the main line of the Menzies of Weem, died in 1918, and the castle then passed through several families. In the 1939-45 war the castle was used as a Polish Army medical supplies depot. The delapidated building was gradually restored by the Menzies Clan Society after they acquired it in 1957.

The castle has a main block 22.6m long by 8.8m wide with square wings set on the SW and NE corners in such a way that each flanks two sides. The entrance in the SW wing is unusually low and retains a yett in front of a studded oak door. It leads into a lobby off which lead a wide circular stair rising the full height of the building, two cellars in the remaining part of the wing, and a doorway onto a passage connecting three cellars and a kitchen with its fireplace in the main block east end wall. Another cellar in the NE wing opens off the kitchen. A few gunports survive at this level. In the 18th century a new doorway was made in the middle of the south front, the easternmost cellar then becoming an entrance lobby with access through to the stairwell of a new wing added on the north side. In 1840 a small Baroque porch with impaled arms of Sir Neil Menzies and Grace Conyers Norton was added in front of the new front doorway. The second storey contains the hall with tiny service rooms at its west end with a private room over the kitchen. The third and fourth storeys were similarly divided, and there were various bedrooms contained in the wings. Access to upper rooms at the east end was provided by a stair in a round turret corbelled out by the main crosswall, but this stair was removed when the 18th century range, now removed by the restorers, was added. At the summit are conical-roofed round bartizans on the outermost corners of the wings and the main block. See pages 12 and 89.

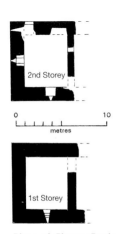

Plans of Cluggy Castle

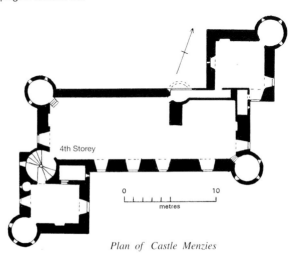

Plan of Castle Menzies

Castle Menzies

CLUGGY   NN 840234

The Comyns had a castle on a promontory on the north side of Monzievaird Loch in the 13th and 14th centuries, and it is said that Malise, Earl of Strathearn was besieged here by that family in 1306. It was referred to as "an ancient fortalice" in 1467 and about that time was given to Patrick, 3rd son of the 6th Baron of Tullibardine, who died here in 1476. The present ruin comprising the 8.4m wide west end of a block of unknown length now two storeys high may be of about that period or rather later. It has a private room over a cellar. Beyond it presumably lay a hall. Sir William Murray, 1st Baronet of Ochtertyre was inhabiting this building in 1650, but his successors built and still occupy a Georgian mansion on the hillside above. There Robert Burns stayed in 1787.

Cluggy Castle

Clunie Castle

CLUNIE   NO 114440 & 111440

On a small wooded island near the south shore of the loch is a castle said to have been built by Bishop Brown of Dunkeld between 1485 and 1514. The main block may be that old but the wing with a kitchen in its basement and the wide round staircase turret in the re-entrant angle are more likely to be the work of Lord Advocate Crichton of Elliock. He was granted Clunie by his kinsman Bishop Crichton in 1562. His son was the celebrated Admirable Crichton. The castle remained roofed until a few decades ago. The stair turret has the unusual feature of a curved gable at the summit.

The Castle Hill (also called The Ward) on the SW side of the loch has low fragments of a massive tower about 15m square at the east end of a platform 90m by 30m wide. This is said to be the site of a palace of Malcolm Canmore. In 1377 Robert II appointed John de Roos keeper of the castle, and the tower may have been built in that period (late 14th century).

COLDOCH   NS 699982

In 1513 James IV granted his tailor Robert Spittal of Stirling the right to build a fortalice here but the existing nucleus of the mansion created by the Grahams seems to be later.

Clunie: Castle Hill or The Ward

Plan of Clunie Castle

Plans of Comrie Castle

Comrie Castle

COMRIE   NN 787487

Near the confluence of the Lyon and Tay is a ruined L-plan tower built by a junior branch of the Menzies family in the late 16th century. An earlier castle on or near this site was the chief seat of the Menzies family until burnt in 1487. The castle has a wing measuring 4.4m by 3.9m overlapping the SW corner of a main block 8.6m long by 6.8m wide. The wing contains a staircase up to the hall, from which rose a narrow stair, now destroyed, over the entrance in the southern re-entrant angle. There are gunports in the single cellar and at the base of the stair. The arch in the second storey north wall is modern.

CORB   NO 164568

Corb is said to have been a hunting seat of the Earls of Crawford, but in the 17th and 18th centuries it was held by the Rattray family, and it was ruined by 1783. All that remains is a mound measuring about 18m by 12m probably covering the base of a tower house.

COWDEN   NS 987997

The large mansion has been demolished but there remains on a rock in the grounds of a new house a roll-moulded courtyard gateway of c1600 with deep draw-bar holes, plus a rather altered polygonal tower bearing the date 1707. There is also what may be part of the base of a round tower.

CRAIGHALL   NO 175480

Craighall was a seat of the Rattrays from the early 16th century. The present mansion is 19th century, except for what appears to be part of a D-shaped tower at the northern end of the promontory high above the gorge of the Ericht. The Statistical Account mentions a second tower and traces of a ditch. The pediment dated 1614 supposedly came from Edinburgh University along with the half-effigy of Bartholomew Somerville (c1640).

DALVEICH   NN 616243

On the north side of Loch Earn is the featureless lower part of a building 28m long by 8m wide, said to have once been a long, low late 16th century Z-plan castle like Glasclune.

DOUNE NN 728011 HS

Doune Castle was built in the 1390s by Robert Stewart, Duke of Albany, Regent of Scotland during the last years of his senile elder brother Robert III. He remained in power during the captivity of the young James I until his own death in 1420. His son Murdoch, 2nd Duke then ruled Scotland until James returned in 1424 and soon struck against several overmighty subjects. Murdoch and his son Alexander and his father-in-law the Earl of Lennox were all executed in 1425 on charges of unconstitutional violence. Doune then became a royal castle and was frequently used as a hunting seat by James II. It was also used as a dower-house and Mary of Gueldres, Margaret of Denmark and Margaret Tudor, the respective consorts of James II, James III and James IV, all spent much of their widowhood in residence at Doune. Margaret Tudor married as her third husband Sir James Stewart, a direct descendant of the Duke of Albany, and in 1528 appointed him as Steward and Chamberlain of Menteith and Captain of Doune Castle.

In 1570 the castle was held for the exiled Queen Mary against the Regent Lennox, but was surrendered without bloodshed after a three day blockade. Later the same year its keeper Sir James Stewart, son of Margaret Tudor's husband, was created Lord Doune. His son, another James, married a daughter of Regent Moray and in 1592 was created Earl of Moray by James VI. The king used the castle occasionally, and in 1581 spent over £300 on repairs to it, but Doune gradually became regarded as the seat of its hereditary keepers. In 1593 James VI got to hear of a plot against himself being hatched within the castle walls. He arrived suddenly and arrested the earls of Montrose and Gowrie, although the Earl of Atholl escaped northwards to his castle at Blair.

Montrose occupied the castle in April 1645 and during Glencairn's rising of 1654 there was a skirmish here between a royal force under Sir Mungo Murray and a detachment of Cromwellian cavalry under Major Bridges. In 1689 the government of William III garrisoned the castle against Viscount Dundee and ordered repairs to the roofs, doors and windows. In the 1745 Jacobite rebellion the castle was seized by the Jacobites and used as a prison to incarcerate government troops taken at Falkirk. Several of them confined in the so-called Queen Mary's room two storeys above the kitchen escaped down from the battlements by means of a rope made from blankets. By this time the castle was in a poor state of repair. It was roofless by 1800, but in the 1880s the 14th Earl of Moray had it re-roofed.

Doune Castle

Doune Castle

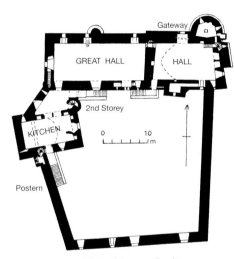

Plan of Doune Castle

Doune Castle lies on a promontory between a tributary burn and the River Teith. The surrounding earthworks may possibly be earlier, but apart from minor repairs and alterations mainly in the form of renewal of parapets, the stonework appears to be all of c1390-1420, a rare instance in Scotland of a building of this size built in a single generation and hardly changed since. It consists of a court 36m across with on the west side a kitchen and various upper rooms and on the north a continuous range formed by a four-storey tower house with the main gateway through its base and a lofty hall over a range of cellars to the west. There are round open bartizans on all the corners of the towers and upon the 2m thick and 12m high curtain wall, where they also occur in a midwall position. Footings of former inner walls and embrasures at second storey level in the south curtain indicate two storey ranges were intended around the other sides of the court, although these were never built.

The tower house is of rather irregular shape and measures about 18m by 13m. It has a rectangular projection on the south side, another on the east rising up as a high lookout turret with a maximum height of almost 29m, and a round tower filling the east half of the north front, flanking the facade and containing various polygonal rooms over a round cellar. The entrance passage is cobbled and still closed by a pair of iron outer gates. Originally there was another pair at the inner end which closed against the court. The rooms on either side could only be reached from above by a hatch in one of the vaults, and the upper storeys formed a private and secure suite for the duke, being reached by a forestair from the court. The lord's hall or audience chamber on the second storey is a lofty vaulted room with a musicians' gallery at one end and an ususual double fireplace at the other. The doorway through to the great hall to the west has been broken through later. A staircase in the NE corner serves the upper rooms and latrines open off the east side of the round tower, which has three upper levels corresponding to two in the main block. See front cover and page 7.

Kitchen service hatches at Doune

The retainers' hall is reached from the court by its own forestair to a lobby between it and the kitchen. It is an impressive chamber 20m long by 8m wide and 12m high to the apex on the roof, in which is a louvre to emit smoke from a fire in a central hearth. One south window has a mullion and transom and the embrasure contains the head of a service stair from the cellars, and there is another such stair in the NW corner, whilst the stair leading south from the west end window embrasure led up to a musicians' gallery at this end. At 17m by 8m the kitchen tower (see front cover) is large enough to be a tower house in its own right. There is a forestair beside the curtain on south side, where there is a postern gateway commanded by a box-machicolation at wall-walk level. Set over cellars, with which it has no communication, the lofty kitchen is vaulted and has a fireplace the full width of the west end of the room, an oven in the SE corner, and a pair of service hatches opening towards the lobby. The corbelled-out turret staircase fitted with gunports and rising from the service lobby is an addition of 1581 to improve access to a guest suite comprising an audience chamber and two bedrooms. In the middle of the courtyard is a well 18m deep usually containing 3m depth of water.

Yett at Doune Castle

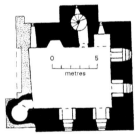

Drummond: plan of tower

DRUMLOCHY   NO 158469

Only a 9m long section of thin walling 4m high and some foundations now remain of a late 16th or early 17th century seat of the Heron family. It or an earlier castle here was destroyed during a feud with the Blairs, whose castle of Glasclune lay just 1km to the west on the other side of a wooden ravine. There are two blocked windows, and a fragment of a round turret with a gunloop. Reset moulded stones lie in the walls of a nearby steading.

Drumlochy Castle

DRUMMOND   NN 844181   G

In 1487 Sir John Drummond of Cargill was created a peer by James III for his services as an ambassador to the English Court and in 1490 he began work on a four storey tower on a rock in the estate then known as Concraig. By a special licence in 1491 James IV authorised the work, and it was named Drummond Castle. It measures about 13m by 11m over walls up to 3m thick and has a staircase turret in the middle of the east side. The king took a fancy to Margaret, eldest daughter of Lord Drummond and his wife Elizabeth Lindsay, and refused to marry anyone else as long as Margaret lived. Nobles advocating a marriage with Margaret Tudor, daughter of Henry VII of England, are thought to have arranged for Margaret Drummond to be poisoned at Drummond Castle, and two other sisters perished with her.

As a reward for negotiating an agreement between James VI and Philip III of Spain, James Drummond was created Earl of Perth in 1605. The 2nd Earl laid out the gardens and built the block at a lower level to the south which contains two storeys of rooms over a gateway flanked by guard-rooms. This block has dormer window pediments dated 1630 and 1636. The 2nd Earl was captured fighting alongside Montrose at the battle of Philiphaugh in 1646 and was heavily fined by Cromwell. The castle became ruinous but after the restoration of Charles II the 3rd Earl built a house on a buttressed terrace east of the court.

The 4th Earl was imprisoned from 1689 to 1693 in Stirling Castle by William III and then went to join James VII in exile, having been created Duke of Perth by him. Both this duke and his son died abroad, but the widow of the 2nd Duke eventually returned to Scotland and resided at Drummond until it was forfeited along with all the estates of the 3rd Duke because of his involvement in the 1745 rebellion. She had the defences dismantled to prevent an occupation by Hanovarian troops and it was probably then that the block lying NE of the tower was reduced to its footings and most of tower north wall destroyed. The Duchess moved to Stobhall, dying there in 1773, aged 90. In 1784 the Drummond estates were granted to Captain James Drummond, then created Baron Perth. His heiress married the son of Lord Gwydir and their son inherited the title Lord Willoughby de Eresby. He patched up the north side of the tower and give it a new roof and battlements. It is now a museum. The family were created earls of Ancaster in 1892 and are still in possession, having rebuilt and enlarged the 17th century house after a fire. See inside front cover.

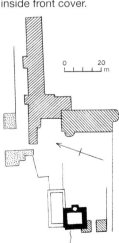

Plan of Drummond Castle   *Drummond Castle*

Duke Murdoch's Castle

DUKE MURDOCH'S NN 473014

On a narrow rocky island on the south side of Lord Ard are low remains of a rectangular building 17m long by 8m wide, which is thought to have been a hunting seat of Murdoch, Duke of Albany, executed in 1425, although it may actually have been built by his father.

DUNBLANE NN 72014 V

Set above a very steep drop to the Allan Water not far SW of the cathedral are remains of the west range of the bishops' palace. Two vaulted rooms remain, above which there was probably once a hall. A fragment of the outer wall also survives of the south range. It is unlikely that any parts of these ruins are older than the period of the three bishops of the Chisholm family who ruled the diocese between 1487 and 1569, but most of the cathedral dates from the mid to late 13th century and the bishops of that period must have had hall and chamber, at least, of stone, and presumably on this site. See picture on page 17.

DUNKELD NO 013424 & 024427

Nothing remains of a tower house built by Bishop Cardney in 1408, or of a chapel and other extensions to the bishops' palace by Bishop Brown. The palace was burnt along with the town by the Jacobites in 1689. To the NE a hotel built c1900 now stands on the site of a house of the Murrays of Blair Atholl. It was stormed and then blown up by Cromwellian troops in 1653, rebuilt in 1679, but demolished in the early 19th century.

DUPPLIN NO 056806

Sir William Oliphant, the heroic defender of Stirling Castle in 1304, had a castle here on a site now occupied by a mansion of 1828-32. The burgesses of Perth destroyed the castles of Aberdalgie and Dupplin in 1461 during a dispute with Lord Oliphant. The castle was rebuilt and in 1623 was sold to William, 8th Earl of Morton. He transferred it to George Hay, then Chancellor, who was created Earl of Kinnoul in 1633. In 1688 Thomas Hay of Balhousie, 6th Earl, rebuilt the north front and added two wings.

Ecclesiamagirdle

Plan of Edinample Castle

Edinample Castle

ECCLESIAMAGIRDLE   NN 107164   V

Beside a small loch is a T-plan house and court with a circular dovecot at one corner. Over the badly leaning courtyard gateway is the date 1648 and initials of Sir David Carmichael of Balmedie and his wife. They are said to have built the house c1629. The estate had been church property (hence the name) and then was sold to the Halyburtons of Pitcur. The entrance doorway lies in the outer wall of the wing containing a staircase linking all three storeys of the main block. The lowest storey is vaulted. The dormer windows of the top storey are Victorian restorations. A turret stair leads to a garret room over the main staircase.

EDINAMPLE   NN 601226

Restored in the 1980s, this castle lies amongst trees near where the Ample Burn runs into the south side of Loch Earn. The main block 15m long by 8.2m wide has corner bartizans and may possibly incorporate parts of a 15th century tower of the MacGregors, although it is more likely that the earlier stronghold of this estate lay on the nearby crannog in the loch. In the 1580s the Campbells of Breadalbane erected the present building with circular towers of 6m and 6.8m diameter respectively on the SE and NW corners. The SE tower contains a bottle dungeon in its base, an unusual feature at so late a date. The entrance lies at the foot of a staircase in a round turret in the western re-entrant angle between this tower and the main block. The hall has a fireplace in the south wall, a mural chamber in the NE corner beside the flue from the kitchen fireplace below, and a service stair leading down in the north wall from a doorway which is a later insertion with an added porch in front. From this level stairs to the bedrooms are corbelled out over the eastern re-entrant angles of each tower.

Elcho Castle

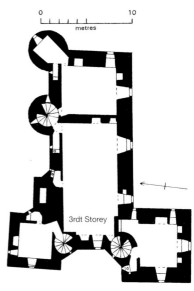

0   10

metres

3rdt Storey

Plan of Elcho Castle

ELCHO   NO 165210   HS

The site of the castle, a rocky knoll overlooking the Tay below Perth, is thought to have been in use since the 13th century, but the present building seems to be mostly the work of Sir John Wemyss of Wemyss, who died in 1572. This family had obtained the estate in 1468. One circular tower which is all that remains of a courtyard to the south bears the initials E.I.W for Earl John Wemyss, who succeeded as laird in 1622, was later made an earl, and lived until 1649. The castle decayed after David, Lord Elcho fled to France after taking part in the 1745 rebellion. It was re-roofed in 1830 and became a state momument in 1929. The main house stands empty but complete with roofs and some of the original grilles over the upper windows. The main block 21m long by 9m contains a main hall and a private room to the east on each of three upper levels over a vaulted basement containing a kitchen at the west end and and two cellars. There are several gunports around the base of the walls. The kitchen has a large fireplace in a projection from the north wall rising the full height of the building. A circular turret beside the main crosswall contains a staircase serving all four levels and at the NE corner is another round turret containing square rooms set diagonally to the main block, the uppermost room being within a square caphouse. On the SE corner a conical-roofed circular bartizan is boldly corbelled out. Square towers engage the western corners, each flanking two walls. Both have turret stairs corbelled out between them and the west wall to serve numerous bedrooms. The NW tower has six storeys, whilst the larger SW tower contains a wide staircase from the entrance to the main hall, two bedrooms above, and then an attic within an ashlar parapet with circular corner bartizans roofed with slabs to create sentry-boxes. See illustrations on pages 12 and 15.

ERROL   NO 246227

The original castle has gone and much of the present mansion dates from after a fire of 1874. William the Lion granted the estate to his butler, William de la Haye. Sir Gilbert Hay of Errol was a staunch supporter of Robert Bruce and was made hereditary High Constable. In 1452 the 9th chief, William, was created Earl of Errol by James II. The Hays retain the titles but transferred their chief seat to Slains in 1634.

EVELICK   NO 205259

Andrew Lindsay of Evelick, a descendant of Earl Beardie (see page 56), was made a baronet in 1666. His second son Thomas was murdered here by his step-brother James Douglas. The victim is said to have been stabbed five times, then held under water, and then finished off by his head being crushed by a rock. The line died out when the last of them drowned in 1799. Much of the shell of a late 16th century L-plan tower house remains, although the features are mostly ragged holes. There is a circular staircase tower in the re-entrant angle. The three storey main block is 11.5m long by 7.4m wide over walls 1.3m thick. there are signs of a destroyed later extension. The wing is 6.2m square and had three levels of upper roomns over a kitchen. There are several gunports in the basement, which was originally vaulted.

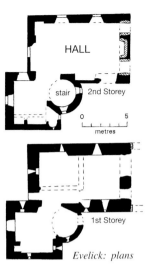

Evelick: plans

FINGASK   NO 228275

The castle consists of a much altered L-plan tower of the 1590s with lower additions of 1675 to the west, and a modern north wing lying on a south-facing terrace above a ravine. It was built by the Bruces, but sold to the Threiplands of Kilbuchno in Peebleshire in the 17th century. Patrick Threipland was Provost of Perth in 1665 and was knighted in 1674 for his work in suppressing the Covenanters. His son Sir David joined forces with the Earl of Mar in 1715 and entertained The Old Chevalier at Fingask in 1716, after which it was occupied by Hanovarian troops and forfeited. Lady Threipland managed to lease Fingask back, but it was again forfeited after the 1745 rebellion, when one son was killed at Prestonpans and another escaped to France with Prince Charles. This son eventually became a successful physician in Edinburgh and repurchased Fingask in 1783, whilst the baronetcy was restored to the family in 1826. Thirty years or so ago the family regained possession of the castle. A square stair turret in the re-entrant angle has gone but there remain several gunports, including one in the fireplace of the kitchen in the base of the wing. Some of the upper windows still retain their original protective iron grilles.

Evelick Castle

Fingask Castle

Finlarig Castle

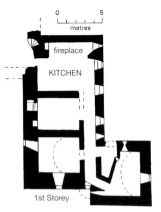

Plan of Finlarig Castle

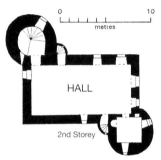

Plan of Gartartan Castle
(*see also page 12*)

Plan of Fordel

FINLARIG   NN 575338   F

Hidden in trees on a low mound protected by the rivers Lochay and Dochart at the west end of Loch Tay is a ruinous Z-plan castle said to have been one of seven castles built by Sir Colin Campbell of Glenorchy. This one lies on land previously held by the Menzies family. A tree-clad motte and bailey platform lie closeby to the north. The castle has a main block 16.4m long by 8.9m wide from which projected two 6.8m square wings giving all-round flanking fire from gunloops. A dumb-bell shaped loop covers the entrance in the SW surviving wing, above which is a panel with the date 1609 and the Royal Arms. From the lobby inside the entrance there was access to a passage leading past two cellars to a kitchen at the far end. A wide stair led up over another cellar in the wing to the now very ruined main hall. From that level a stair was corbelled out over the west re-entrant angle. Little remains of the other wing apart from a service stair to the hall up from a fourth cellar reached from the kitchen.

Fordel

FORDEL   NO 143124

Below a farm are a group of ruins probably dating from c1600-40. At the east end of a ground-floor hall 9.5m wide by 4.8m wide with a deep fireplace recess on the north side is a block measuring 9.4m by 6.2m over walls 1m thick. It contained a dark unvaulted basement, an upper storey probably divided into two since there are fireplaces at each end, and an attic room in the roof. At the NW corner of this block is a round turret with a gunloop under the foot of a staircase rising from an entrance doorway. West of the hall is another private room with a fireplace in front of the west wall. There are remains of two other buildings nearby.

GARTARTAN   NS 530978

Near a more recent mansion lies a Z-plan castle probably built by Malcolm McFarlane, who in 1597 made a bond of mutual support against enemies with John, Earl of Menteith. Walter McFarlane of Ardleish had obtained the half of the estate belonging to John Lyle in 1531. The castle was allowed to decay after it passed to the Grahams of the neighbouring estate of Gartmore, although it was at least partly habitable in the late 19th century. The main block is 13m long by 7.3m wide and has round towers 5.2m in diameter engaging the east and west corners. Both have turret stairs corbelled out above the re-entrant angles they make with the main side walls, and one contains a wide circular stair from the entrance to the hall. There is no fireplace in the hall, and little survives of the upper rooms. One end of the hall was screened off as an ante-room and has a hatch in the floor for access to the vaulted cellar below.

Gartartan Castle

Garth Castle

Last remains of Gascon Hall

GARTH   NN 764504

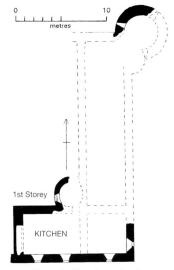

Strongly situated between the ravines of two branches of the Keltney Burn is a plain and massive tower of early date with a straight stair rising from one side of the entrance in the middle of the north wall.   It probably existed by 1394 when here died Alexander Stewart, an illegitimate son of Robert II nicknamed The Wolf of Badenoch for his lawless deeds, which included burning Elgin Cathedral during a feud with its bishop. In 1502 a descendant, Nigel Stewart, burnt the seat of the chief of the Menzies clan and starved him in the dungeon at Garth until he signed away some of his rights. Nigel was later accused of murdering his own wife and he ended up a prisoner for nine years in his own stronghold until he died in 1554. Garth then passed to Stewart of Drumcharry. The tower was inhabited until the late 18th century but most of one wall had to be rebuilt when it was restored from ruin in the 1880s for Sir Donald Currie. In the 1960s the tower was again made habitable from an advanced state of decay.

Plan of Glasclune Castle

GASK   NN 986175 & 995189

A fragment of the stair turret of the early 17th century mansion of Gascon Hall lies close to the River Earn. Just 2km away is the mansion of Old Gask, almost completely rebuilt since being destroyed by Hanovarian troops in 1746 because Lord Oliphant was a Jacobite. Only in 1757 was his heir allowed to succeed to the title. The Oliphants are now at Ardblair.

GLASCLUNE   NO 154470

Glasclune was a seat of a branch of the Blairs that fought a long feud with the Herons of Drumlochy on the other side of a ravine of a tributary of the Lornty Burn. The castle had a 24.7m long and 6m wide main block, now mostly destroyed. On the NW corner was a round tower 6.8m in diameter, still nearly intact with a stair-turret in the NE re-entrant angle a century ago, but now reduced to a fragment. Another fragment remains of the private rooms at the south end of the main block, with corbelling for a round corner bartizan. Adjoining this end is a wing containing a private room over a kitchen. There are gunloops below the windows and part of a stair turret in the re-entrant angle, facing towards where there was a court.

GLENDEVON   NN 976055

The main block of this plain whitewashed Z-plan building has walls up to 2.7m thick and may go back to the time of William, 8th Earl of Douglas, who is thought to have used it as a hunting serat. The wings were added by the Crawfords, probably in the 1590s. The date 1766 and the initial R refer to the Rutherfords, later owners. The building has been much altered but the separate entrances into the SW wing and the main block and a lack of any lower doorway between these parts seems to be original. A later extension hides the doorway into the wing. A stair turret projects out where this wing meets the main block. The eastern extension containing a vaulted basement is probably 17th century.

Glasclune Castle (see also page 16)

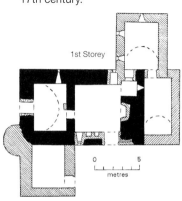

1st Storey

0   5
metres

Plan of Glendevon Castle

Glendevon Castle

Gleneagles Castle

GLENDOICK   NO 208237

Part of a late 16th century house built by Sir Thomas Murray, Lord Clerk Register, survives at the back of the lofty white-washed mansion built by Lord President Robert Craigie in the 18th century.

GLENEAGLES   NN 929093

A knoll beside a ravine near the late 17th century mansion bears fragments of a heart-shaped court 45m across with the lower part of a large tower house in the middle and traces of outbuildings on the west. Probably built by the Haldanes in the early 16th century, but possibly only a remodelling of a 14th century structure, the tower measures 17.3m by 11.8m over walls 2.1m thick and seems to have had its unvaulted basement divided into several cellars and a kitchen. The low vaulted room above must have been a hall or mess-room for retainers. Nothing remains of the upper levels, which were probably subdivided. There are remains of a staircase in the SE corner. The estate passed to the Duncans in 1799.

Gleneagles Castle

Grandtully Castle (see also page 15)

*Plan of
Grandtully Castle*

Plans of Gleneagles Castle

GRANDTULLY   NN 891513

The present Steuart-Fotheringham owners are de-scended from Alexander, 4th High Steward of Scot-land, who held lands here in the 14th century. The nearly square (10.2m by 9.4m) four storey main block of the Z-plan may be late 14th or 15th century, at least in its lower parts. The five storey 6m square wings are late 16th century, or possibly as late as 1626, the date set upon the building with initials of Sir William Stewart, Sheriff of Perth, and his wife Dame Agnes Moncrieffe. There are conical-roofed bartizans and one wing has an unusually late example of a corbelled-out latrine. This wing has a lofty round stair turret with an ogival cap in the smaller of two re-entrant angles between it and the main block. The entrance lies in the other re-entrant angle. A kitchen once probably lay on the second sto-rey of this wing, but another has been created in the other wing at a later date. The castle lies in a position of strategic importance and was used successively as a headquarters by Montrose in the 1640s, General Mackay in 1689, the Earl of Argyll in the 1690s, the Earl of Mar in the 1715 rebellion, and Prince Charles in the 1745 rebellion. One of Mackay's officers is said to have been shot dead in one of the bartizan closet rooms. in the 19th century Grandtully became derelict when the family abandoned it in favour of Murthly, but it was in use again by the 1890s, when a new wing was added, and in the 1920s Admiral Beatty had a tenancy of the castle for shooting holidays.

HUNTINGTOWER   NO 084251   HS

The estate was originally called Ruthven and was long held by a family that from the early 13th century onwards took their name from it. The earliest parts of the castle may go back to the time of Sir William Ruthven, one of the hostages sent to England in the 1420s as security for the ransom of James I. It then comprised a court surrounded by a wall about 1.2m thick which was entered through a passage in the eastern part of the basement of a tower house measuring 11.2m by 7.4m on the south side. It was perhaps his great-grandson William, created Lord Ruthven in 1489, who remodelled the tower, blocking up the old gateway passage and providing new west and north walls with a spiral staircase in the NW corner, an entrance at ground level, and numerous upper windows with seats in the embrasures. The lowest two storeys have fireplaces in the north wall and the top storey entirely of this era has a fireplace in the east wall, a latrine in the SW corner and an aumbry beside the staircase. There is an attic within a wall-walk with a corbelled parapet with small angle-rounds.

It may have been William, 2nd Lord Ruthven, who married the heiress Janet Halyburton of Dirleton in East Lothian, who built a second tower-like block of similar size just 2.7m away to the west. A modern forestair leads to the entrance at second storey level beside a stair in a round NW turret. Overlapping the SW corner is a wing rising one storey higher than the three of the main block. It has an attic dovecot within a wall-walk with angle-rounds. North of this second tower, filling much of the west side of the former court, was a single storey hall block with large windows and a fireplace at the north end. Ruins of it still stood when Captain Robert Grose made a drawing of the castle in 1790.

William, 4th Lord Ruthven, who was implicated along with his father in the murder of Queen Mary's favourite Riccio at Holyrood in 1566, served as Treasurer of Scotland in 1571 and was created Earl of Gowrie by the teenage James VI in 1581. In the following year the earl and several other lords seized King James in Perth and brought him to Ruthven Castle in what became known as the "Raid of Ruthven". The Earl of Arran, then effectively in power, was captured and imprisoned in the castle the next day. For nearly a year Gowrie and his fellow conspirators ruled Scotland until James escaped. In 1583 he issued a proclamation pardoning those connected with the raid, and in 1584 he stayed at the castle for a week of hunting, but in 1585 Gowrie was executed on a charge of plotting to seize Stirling Castle. An act of forfeiture was rescinded in 1586. John, 3rd Earl of Gowrie and his brother Alexander were killed in their town house in Perth in 1600 on the grounds that they were plotting against King James. On the earl's dead body were found magical writings confirming the family involvement in necromancy and witchcraft. In November that year the family were forfeited and the surname and placename of Ruthven abolished, the barony and castle being offically renamed Huntingtower.

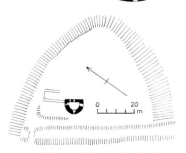

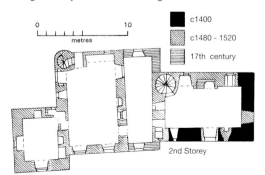

Plan of Huntingtower Castle   *Plans of Inchbervie Castle*

Huntingtower Castle

The castle remained with the Crown until Charles I granted it in 1643 to William Murray, then created Earl Dysart and Lord Huntingtower. The castle was sold to a kinsman, James Murray, Earl of Tullibardine in 1663, after whose death it passed to the Murray earl of Atholl. At some point in the 17th century a narrow block was built between the two towers, some of their windows and fireplaces were altered, and each part was given a new entrance at ground level in the south wall. A dowager duchess of Atholl resided at Huntingtower in the 1760s. Charles Pennant, who visited the castle c1780 was told a story which he relates about a daughter of the 1st Earl of Gowrie who is said to have leapt across the 2.7m gap between the east and west towers in order to escape being caught in her lover's room. In later years the castle was used by a colony of halico printers and in 1912 was handed over to the state for preservation. During restoration work painted murals and a tempera-painted ceiling of c1540 were revealed in the second storey room of the east tower. Other paintings can be seen in the embrasure of a window in the second storey of the wing of the west tower.

INCHBERVIE   NO 123329

On a wooded peninsular in a bend of the Tay is a D-shaped enclosure measuring 60m by 38m. The straight side faces to landward and has a ditch in front of it. Near the middle of this side is the lowest stage of a mid 16th century D-shaped tower 11m in diameter over walling 3m thick pierced by gunloops commanding the ditch. The basement is still vaulted. Little remains of other buildings, although there was an inhabited mansion here until it was burned in 1887. At the Reformation the lands here passed from Dunfermline Abbey to the Nairne family. The 3rd Lord Nairne narrowly escaped capture here after the 1746 rebellion.

Inchbervie Castle

Innerpeffray Castle

Plan of Kilbryde

INCHBRACKIE   NN 903218

Only an elongated moated enclosure now covered in trees and a few scattered stones now remain of a castle of the Graham family destroyed by Cromwell in 1650.

INNERPEFFRAY   NN 905179

The ruined castle lies on low ground near the River Earn far from the medieval church and any road. It is a spacious but plain L-plan building built in the early 17th century by James Drummond, 1st Lord Madderty, a younger brother of the 3rd Lord Drummond, for whom as an infant, the lands of Inchaffray Abbey had been made a temporal lordship at the Reformation. The main block measuring 17.6m by 8.3m contained a hall over several cellars and bedrooms above which were partly in the roof. The wing is higher, having contained three storeys of private rooms over a kitchen with a gunloop covering the entrance. A square turret within the re-entrant angle contained a stair linking all the rooms.

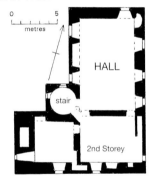

Plan of Innerpeffray Castle
See also page 12.

INVERMAY   NO 061163

Beside a large Georgian mansion lies the late 16th century L-plan tower built by Alexander Belshes, who obtained the estate by marrying the heiress of Thomas Murray. The tower has a caphouse over a stair wing which is reached by a small turret-stair and a keyhole shaped loop guards the entrance. The turret in the middle of the opposite side from the wing was added in 1633, the date that appears upon it.

INVERQUIECH   NO 277497

A rocky platform 85m long by 25m wide lies above the junction of the Burn of Quiech with the River Isla, with a natural gully protecting the north side. Towards the north end are three fragments of walling about 1.5m thick and 5m high which are relics of an early courtyard castle in which Edward I stayed in 1296. Robert II made his nephew James Lindsay keeper of the then ruinous castle in 1394. A gunloop in one fragment indicates the site was still in use in the 16th century. There are two other framents facing the river, one with a fireplace and latrine and the other containing a postern gateway.

Invermay

Keltie Castle

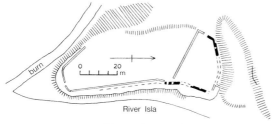

Plan and view of Inverquiech Castle

KEIR   NN 770989

In 1448 Lucas de Stirling obtained Keir from Leslie of that Ilk and his descendants still own it, despite temporary forfeiture for their part in the rebellions of 1715 and 1745. The house is a composite of various periods, considerable parts being added by Sir William Stirling-Maxwell, who succeeded in 1865 to the barony of Pollock. Much of the house is 18th century but part of it may go back to the mid or late 15th century.

KELTIE   NO 008133

This late 16th century L-plan tower is unusual in having a square bartizan set below, rather than at, roof level. In it are five gunloops. Several second storey windows have been enlarged, but one which is still covered by a grille must be original. There are modern attic dormer windows. Keltie belonged to the Bonars from the early 15th century but was sold in 1692 to John Drummond of Culdees, one lintel having his initials and the year 1712. David, son of the 8th Earl of Airlie married the heiress Clementina Drummond in 1812. The castle was sold to Lord Rollo in 1833.

KILBRYDE   NN 756036

The castle is strongly sited by a bend of the ravine of the Ardoch Burn. Parts of it are 19th century but much of it is early 17th century and has square bartizans on three of the corners. Above vaulted cellars and a kitchen are two levels which contained private rooms beyond halls, and there are bedrooms in the roof. An earlier castle here was built by Sir James Graham in 1460. Kilbryde was sold to Sir Colin Campbell of Aberuchill, Lord Justice Clerk in 1669. He and his successor Sir James were obliged to pay blackmail to Rob Roy MacGregor for fear of losing their flocks of sheep. See page 11.

KILSPINDIE   NO 219258

William Wallace and his mother took refuge in a castle here according to the account by Blind Harry. The later castle successively owned by the Crawfords and Lindsays was dismantled in 1840. The only relics of it are two stones built into a manse outhouse nearby. One has what may be the Douglas heart quartered with the arms of either the Stewarts or Lindsays (it is very worn). The building had a long main body with chambers at either end of a hall set over a basement containing three cellars and a kitchen at the west end all linked by a passage on the north side to a staircase in the re-entrant angle between the main block and a NW wing. There was a section of open wall-walk on the west end of the main block but it is not clear how access to it was obtained.

KINCARDINE   NO 946110

Near a farm some way SW of the modern castle are slight traces of a quadrangular castle of the Grahams from which the Duke of Montrose takes the secondary title of Earl of Kincardine. It was dismantled by the Marquess of Argyll in 1645 and probably never restored.

KINCLAVEN   NO 158377

Hidden in trees by the junction of the Tay and the Isla is a court measuring 35m by 36m inside a wall 2.2m thick and 6m high. At each corner is a ruined narrow passage to the lowest level of a destroyed tower of unknown shape and size. On the west is a gateway which seems to have been closed by a portcullis and a staircase to the wall-walk. A buttress hides the outer opening of a dog-leg shaped postern passage on the south. The more accessible west and north sides are protected by a ditch some way from the walls. The castle was probably built by Alexander II c1230-40. One of his documents dated 1264 mentions wine being provided here and the repair of a boat. Edward I stayed in the castle in 1296, and three years later it was captured and wrecked by William Wallace. English royal forces captured the castle in 1335 but it was captured and destroyed by the Scots in 1336. It may have been repaired yet again and possibly still served as a royal castle until the mid 15th century.

KINFAUNS   NO 151226

A Gothic mansion of 1822 designed by Sir Robert Smirke lies on the site of a fortalice of the Charteris family, supposedly descended from a French pirate named Thomas de Longueville who settled in Scotland and supported Robert Bruce. Several of this family served as provosts of Perth. The property later passed to the Blairs and then went to the 12th Lord Grey.

Kinclaven Castle

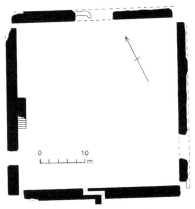

Plan of Kinclaven Castle

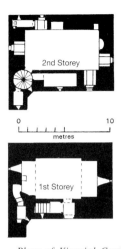

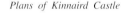

Plans of Kinnaird Castle

Kinnaird Castle

KINGSEAT   NO 147545

Kingseat house is mostly 19th century but a thinly walled wing measuring 7m by 5m from an L-plan 17th century house survives within the south wing. A gunloop and four yetts are incorporated in the garden walls. Kinseat is shown on maps of c1600 and c1750.

KINNAIRD   NO 242291   V

On a promontory above a stream stands a lofty sandstone late 15th century tower and a detached kitchen wing nearby bearing the date 1610, so it was fairly new when James VI stayed for several days' hunting in 1617. It also has initials of Sir Patrick Threipland, 1st Baronet of Fingask, who purchased the castle in 1674. The estate had earlier belonged to the Kinnaird family supposedly descended from Randolph Rufus, who is said to have settled here in the 1170s. The original castle was destroyed after its capture by the Earl of Angus following the murder of John Auchinleck by Sir Robert Colville of Kinnaird in 1449. The kitchen has a fireplace 4m wide and a serving hatch to the outside. The tower has four storeys below the corbelled parapet and an attic added in the late 19th century, when a later Sir Patrick Threipland restored it from ruin. It measures 11.5m long by 8.2m wide and is 18m high to the parapet top. A distinctive feature is the buttress-turret at the SW corner strengthening the wall where there is a spiral stair, off which, leading through the buttress, is a passage to the wall-walk of a vanished barmkin wall. In the corner behind the base of the buttress is a pit-prison. The three uppermost storeys all have latrines in the NW corner, window embrasures with seats, and rooms big enough to take beds within the middle of the south wall.

KINNOULL   NO 123228

Part of this seat of the Hays remained until the late 18th century. George Hay was created first a knight and then a lord by James VI, and Charles I elevated him as Earl of Kinnoull, so he probably had a substantial house here.

KINVAID   NO 063300

A farmhouse lies on the site of a castle said to have been built by Bishop Brown of Dunkeld in the 15th century. It was later the home of Bessie Bell and Mary Gray, two friends whose death from plague in 1645 is commemorated in a well-known traditional folk song.

LAIGHWOOD   NO 077457

A mound rising 2m to a summit 63m by 55m located SE of the farm is said to be the site of an early 14th century castle of Bishop William Sinclair. In the late 18th century two vaults with parts of loopholes survived, and vestiges of two other ranges and a surrounding moat.

LANRICK   NN 685031

The house demolished in 2002 after being derelict for fifty years was mostly early to mid 19th century with an 18th century nucleus. Once held by the Haldanes of Gleneagles it later passed to the MacGregors, and then was sold to the tea-merchant William Jardine.

LENY   NS 613089

The original L-plan building of c1600 has been altered and extended into a large mansion and only the east side with a crow-stepped gable survives more or less in its original state. On the north side the building bears the arms of the Buchanans, owners until the 1940s (see page 13). Francis Buchanan was hanged in 1746 after Stewart of Glenbuckie, leader of a party of Stewarts on their way to join the Jacobite army, was found shot through the head after accepting an invitation to stay at Leny en-route.

LETHENDY   NO 140417

At the side of a large Victorian sandstone mansion is an L-plan tower of c1600 with two full storeys and an attic over a vaulted cellar and kitchen. A gunloop covers the doorway, over which is a panel with the date 1678 and the arms of the Herons. The south gable of the wing has been refaced and two large buttresses added to the main block south wall. Above the vaults the sidewalls are offset externally, perhaps evidence of a pause in construction or the survival of older work lower down.

LOCH BEANIE   NO 160686

In the middle of the loch is a square artificial island with traces of walling. Pont's map of c1600 has a mansion here marked as being the seat of the laird of Glenshie and Strathardle, but it is not shown on Roy's map of c1750.

Lethendy   *Logie*

Loch Dochart: plan

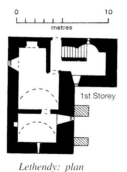

1st Storey

Lethendy: plan

Loch Dochart Castle

LOCH DOCHART   NN 406257

On an island in the loch are ruins of one of several castles built by Sir Duncan Campbell between 1585 and 1631. It was burned in 1646. The main block 13.2m long by 6.6m wide was entered on the north side and divided into a large kitchen and a small room, above which was a private room reached by a turret stair on the north side. A second stair on the south side served the rooms over the kitchen, but only a boldly projecting chimney-breast on the south side now stands higher than the lowest level. The tiny room in the circular SE turret does not communicate with the rest of the building and must have been a pit-prison.

LOCH EARN   NN 690243

Hidden under vegetation on an island near the east end of the loch are slight remains of a castle of the Neishes. After their defeat in battle at Glenboltachan a few Neishes held out here until the twelve sons of the chief of the Macnabs crossed the mountains from Tayside with a boat and captured the island. The MacNabs commemorated this event by adopting an image of the head of the Neish chief then killed as the heraldic crest of their own chief.

LOGIE   NN 014297

This ruined mansion on the north bank of the Almond was demolished in the 1960s except for one lofty round tower containing gunloops commanding the river. A three storey 16th or 17th century block adjoining the tower became the south range of a court with buildings on the other three sides erected by Sir John Drummond, 4th son of the 2nd Earl of Perth. A detached additional north range was added in the late 18th century by Sir William Drummond. The Murray Earl of Mansfield now owns the estate.

LOGIERAIT   NN 977513

A ditch and a few traces of the footings of walls hidden in undergrowth are all that remain of a castle of Robert III set on a strong peninsular site near the junction of the Tay and Tummel. A memorial to the 6th Duke of Atholl lies on the site. The castle had a hall 20m long with galleries at both ends. Rob Roy MacGregor escaped from confinement here in 1717, and in 1745 the Jacobite army used the castle to confine 600 prisoners captured at Prestonpans.

MAINS   NN 668360

Of this Campbell castle on a promontory on the south side of Loch Tay there remain only the lower parts of a long thin-walled rectangular building of uncertain date and purpose.

Meggernie Castle   *Megginch Castle*

MEGGERNIE   NN 554460   V

Adjoining a mansion on flat haugh-land is a five storey tower with pyramidal roofed square bartizans, walls 1.5m thick, a south facing entrance, and gunloops below the upper windows. It was built c1580 either by the Menzies of Culdares, who owned much of the land of Glen Lyon, or by Colin Campbell, who is said to have hekl here the abducted Countess of Erroll. One of the turret rooms is supposed to be haunted by the murdered wife of a Menzies chief. The estate was later held by the Stewarts of Cardney but was sold in 1885.

MEGGINCH   NO 242246

Megginch was a Hay seat from early times until 1664, when it was sold by Sir George Hay to John Drummond, 8th Lord Lennoch, Hereditary Seneschal of Strathearn, whose descendants still live there. The core of the sandstone mansion is an early 16th century tower with wide gunports and several mural chambers and passages in the thick walls. In a remodelling of 1575, that date appearing on it, a circular stair turret with a square caphouse was added on one side which still retains an open wall-walk and one conical-roofed bartizan. Alterations were made in 1707 and a Robert Adam wing added in 1790, whilst further work was done in 1820 and 1928. The later parts required restoration after a fire in 1969. A long-forgotten brick-vaulted passage leading south under the drive was discovered when part of it collapsed under the weight of a fire-engine.

MENTEITH or INCH TULLA   NN 572004

On wooded Inch Tulla in the Lake of Menteith are overgrown ruins of the original chief seat of the earldom of Menteith. In the mid 13th century the earldom passed by marriage from the original Celtic line to Walter Stewart. Another heiress brought it to Robert Stewart, Duke of Albany, brother of Robert III, and the builder of Doune Castle (see page 94). In 1427 Malise Graham became the first of a new line of earls of Menteith, and his descendants retained the title until deprived of it by Charles I, although they were given a new, less attractive earldom of Airth in exchange. With Doune retained by the crown Inch Tulla remained occupied by the earls until c1700, when Katherine Bruce, wife of the then earl, refused to live on the island because of the damp. The oldest building is a two storey chamber block on the south side of the court. It has holes for the beams of a timber gallery on the south side. West of it is a late 16th or 17th century kitchen with windows thought to be reset from Inchmahome Priory, which lies on a neighbouring island. Only the outer wall remains of the west range. On the north side of the court are remains of a hall. Offices and stables lay on the shore nearby.

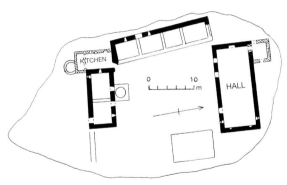

Plan of Inch Tulla, Lake Menteith

Methven Castle

METHVEN   NO 042261   V

The present five storey structure 17.5m long by 14.5m long with unusually regular window patterns is mostly the work of Esme Stewart, Duke of Lennox, who was given Methven in 1584, and his son Ludovick. Both were favourites of James VI. John Mylne of Dundee is thought to have been the architect. The conical-roofed corner turrets rising the full height of the building are additions, only being bonded in at the top. The entrance in the west front is covered by a gunloop in the NW turret, and has above it a small platform.

The southern half appears to incorporate a hall used by Margaret Tudor, sister of Henry VIII of England and wife of James IV. After he was killed at Flodden she married Henry Stewart of Ochiltree, getting him enobled as Lord Methven. She died here in 1542. The spine wall may be partly still older, since Walter, Earl of Atholl had a castle here at the time of his execution for treason in 1427. The castle was then obtained by Sir William Crichton, but was forcibly taken from him in 1444. James II and his queen resided here in 1450-1. The castle was sold in 1664 to Patrick Smythe of Braco. A stone with initials of Patrick and his wife Ann Keith was found during alterations. The Smythes sold Methven to James Cox in 1923. Extensions of 1792, 1800 and 1813 were mostly demolished in the 1950s and 1980s, when the building was restored after many years of neglect.

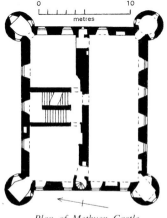

Plan of Methven Castle

Methven Castle

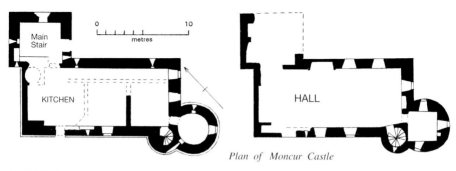

Plan of Moncur Castle

MONCUR   NO 284295

In the estate of Lord Kinnaird's seat of Rossie Park is the ruined original seat of the family. They transferred to Drummie after Moncur was gutted by fire in the 18th century, before returning to build Rossie Park. Moncur is a Z-plan castle of c1580 with gunports on the lowest of three storeys. The main block is 17.4m long by 8.2m wide and contained a kitchen with a fireplace and oven at the NW end and two cellars connected by a passage to the entrance and main stair in the square wing on the north corner. The round tower on the south corner has a circular cellar and then square private rooms above. Within its west re-entrant angle is a turret containing a stair from the wine cellar up to what was probably a private room divided off at this end of the hall. The stair continued up to serve the bedrooms at this end. A tall chimney stack still rises over the hall fireplace on the NE side. The main block third storey was partly in the roof, but the tower and wing rose to a slightly higher level.

MONZIE   NN 873245

At the back of the large and lofty castellated early 19th century mansion is a low three storey L-plan building with gunloops, heraldry and panelling. It was probably one of the castles built c1600-20 by Sir Duncan Campbell of Glenorchy. The date 1634 perhaps refers to either completion or modifications by his fifth son Archibald, whose descendants held Monzie until 1869. There are an extraordinary number of sundials on the window jambs. The castle was restored c1900 by Sir Robert Lorimer and now belongs to the Maitland-MacGill-Crichtons.

Moncur Castle

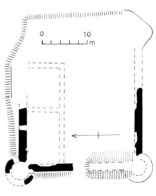

Plan of Moulin Castle

Moulin Castle

MOREDUN HALL   NO 145193

Only a fragment remains of the NE corner of Moredun Hall, a 16th century house of the Moncreiffe family, here since at least the mid 13th century. The present mansion of Moncreiffe House some way to the west was built just after its late 17th century predecessor was burnt down in 1957, killing the 23rd laird. Just one doorway survives of that building. The family now live at Easter Moncreiffe, not far east of the site of Moredun Hall.

MOULIN   NN 946589

Fragments remain of the 1.7m thick walls which enclosed a court measuring 28m by 23.6m of a castle built in 1326 by Sir John Campbell, later created Earl of Atholl by David II. The site was originally an island in a loch. Known as Caisteal Dubh (Black Castle), it seems to have been abandoned in the 16th century. Two corners have remains of round flanking towers, that to the NW having a pair of very ruined basement loops and being 6.2m in diameter. The SE corner looks as if it had a rectangular building placed diagonally, perhaps a later addition. Foundations of a wall suggest a range 7m wide on the north side of the court.

MURTHLY   NO 070399

Murthly passed from the Abercrombies to Sir William Stewart of Grandtully in 1615, and his descendants the Steuart-Fotheringhams are still there. They became baronets in 1683, but the title became extinct on the death of the 8th baronet in 1890. An L-plan tower of uncertain date forming the nucleus was later given bartizans, perhaps c1617, the date that is thought to be given on the very worn panel on the east side along with the Stewart arms. Wings were later added on either side, and still later each wing was extended and a new central portico added. A large new mansion added in front in the 1830s by Sir William Drummond-Stewart, 6th baronet, was removed in 1949.

Monzie Castle

Murthly Castle

Newton Castle

Rednock Castle

NEWTON   NO 172453

High above Blairgowrie is an early 17th century castle of the Drummonds. It has a main block of three storeys and an attic and at diagonally opposite corners are a square wing and a round tower, both of four full storeys. The round tower contains a dome-vaulted cellar in which local gentlemen are said to have remained safely hidden when the the rest of the castle was burned by Cromwellian troops. Here in 1687 was born George Drummond, six times Lord Provost of Edinburgh. Newton now belongs to the Macphersons of Clunie. See p17.

NEWTON DOUNE   NN 731013

On higher ground east of Doune Castle lies a harled late 16th century L-plan house with the unusual feature of a rounded gable-end to the wing. It was a seat of a branch of the Edmonstones of Duntreath who served the earls of Moray as captains of Doune Castle. In 1708 the then owner of Newton Doune was one of five Perthshire lairds arrested after an abortive Jacobite rising but acquitted after the Lord Advocate mishandled the trial proceedings. A staircase turret lies with the re-entrant angle.

OGILVIE   NO 909081

In a garden are slight remains of a Graham castle in a strong position above a ravine amongst the Braes of Ogilvie at the foot of the Ochil Hills.

OLD KIPPENROSS   NS 785999

On the north gable of the house of c1770 built by the Stirlings of Kippendavie is a panel dated 1617 with the initials A.S. and I.M. The house is in fact built on the vaulted cellars (now only above ground on the south) of a house of about that period (when it belonged to the Pearsons), which was burned down in 1768. The walled garden has a datestone of 1703.

PERTH   NO 120235   V

A castle guarding the bridge over the Tay was destroyed along with it by a flood in 1210. A 15m length of walling in George St is a relic of Cromwell's square fort of 1652 with corner bastions. County Buildings lie on the site of a house of the Countess of Huntly built in 1520 and later sold to the Ruthven Earl of Gowrie. Here in 1600 he plotted to kill James VI, whilst in 1663 the Hay Earl of Kinnoul enterained Charles II in the house. It later served as a cavalry barracks but was demolished in 1805.

PITCASTLE   NN 172554

This small humble ruin was the seat of the Robertsons. It had two rooms on each of two storeys, one of the upper rooms being reached by a forestair, perhaps added later. The largest lower room has a large fireplace. The building was more an ordinary farmhouse than a tower, a drawbar for the door being the ony defensive feature.

PITFOUR   NO 200209

The earls of Crawford held Pitfour in the late 15th century. Most of the existing house is the work of the Stewart-Richardsons of Pencaitland in 1829, but one wing built by the Hays dates from 1784, and there may be a late 16th or early 17th century nucleus.

PITHEAVLIS   NO 097222

This castle by the A93 on the SW outskirts of Perth was probably built immediately after John Ross of Craigie sold the estate to Robert Stewart in 1586. It had passed to the Oliphants by 1636 and was a farmhouse in the late 19th century. Still occupied, it is a well-preserved three storey building with gunloops and two conical-roofed bartizans set on the outer corners of the staircase wing containing the entrance.

REDNOCK   NN 600022

Rednock was and still is a Graham possession. By the approach to the farm is a circular stair turret 4.3m in diameter which once lay at the SW corner of the tower. It is furnished with gunloops.

ROHALLION   NO 039401   F

Amongst crags and bracken on the hillside high above the A9 is a drystone reconstruction of 1974 of the lower part of a tower measuring 8m by 6.2m with diagonally opposite tiny corner round turrets.

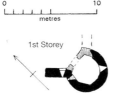

Rohallion: plan   *Rednock: plan*

Rohallion Castle   *Pitheavlis Castle*

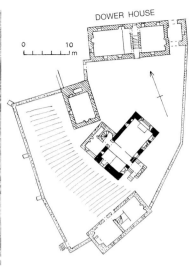

Dower House, Stobhall

Plan of Stobhall

SCONE   NO 113266   OP

The existing mansion of 1803-8 incorporates part of a house thought to an adaptation by the Ruthvens in the 1580s of the house of the abbot of Scone Abbey. A late 16th century outer gateway survives 100m to the east, flanked by ruined circular towers containing gunports. After the Ruthvens were forfeited in 1600 Scone passed to David Murray of Tullibardine, who had helped save the king's life. He was created Baron Scone in 1605 and Viscount Stormont in 1621. His descendants became earls of Mansfield in 1776. Scone was the place of inauguration of the Scottish kings, the last such ceremony being that of Charles II in 1651.

STOBHALL   NO 132344

The Drummonds had a seat here by the 14th century, Robert III's consort Annabella being one of them. After Drummond Castle was built in the 1490s Stobhall was used mostly as a dower-house. It has neither a tower house nor a large mansion but instead are four fairly modest and isolated buildings within a court enclosed by low modern walls perched on a promontory above the Tay. The gatehouse range called the Dowry House now forms the residence of the Drummond chiefs, created earls of perth in 1605 (see page 97). It bears the initials of John, 2nd Earl, who succeeded vin 1612, and his wife Jane, with their arms.The L-shaped chapel block in the middle has the date 1578 on a fireplace lintel of an upper room with initials of David, 2nd Lord Drummond and his wife Dame Lilias Ruthven. However this building, which has a turret stair corbelled out on one side of its wing, is probably a remodelled medieval structure. One north window certainly looks medieval, although it may have been taken from another building. The Bakehouse was built by James, 3rd Duke of Perth, who died on board a ship for France of wounds received fighting on the Jacobite side at Culloden. The fourth block at a lower level containing a laundry is rather later.

STRATHALLAN   NN 919156

Some old work may survive in the existing castellated mansion. It belonged to a branch of the Drummonds created viscounts Strathallan in 1686, the title now being merged with the earldom of Perth. The 4th Viscount, a Jacobite, was mortally wounded at Culloden in 1746.

STRUIE   NO 179114

A stair turret with gunloops remains in the garden of Mains of Struie.

TAYMOUTH   NN 785466 & 766454

Within the present huge mansion of 1801-42 built by the Campbell earls of Breadalbane are reported to survive the vaulted cellars of a Z-plan castle called Balloch built by Sir Colin Campbell of Glenorchy in the 1580s. John Nattes in 1780 depicted it as having bartizans on each of one corner of the main block and the stair wing, and a round tower at the corner diagonally opposite the wing. There were later extensions at either end.

In the late 16th century this branch of the Campbells (created earls of Breadalbane in 1681), also fortified the former nunnery on Eilean nan Bannoamh (The Isle of Female Saints) lying near the north shore of Loch Tay. It was besieged by Montrose in 1645 and was later occupied by General Monk's forces for Cromwell. The remains are hidden by vegetation.

TOM A CHAISTEAL   NN 824216

The last remains of a castle of the Celtic earls of Strathearn on the summit of this tree-clad hill were removed when an obelisk to Sir David Baird was erected on the summit.

TROCHRIE   NO 978402

In a garden behind a house lies the lower parts of the staircase turret of a tower built in the late 16th century by the Ruthven family.

TOMB   NO 121701

A base of a tower remains in a cottage garden.

TULLIBARDINE   NN 910135

It is likely that Sir David Murray, founder of the nearby chapel in 1446, had a tower here, and that other parts were built after his descendants were made earls of Tullibardine in 1606. This branch became marquesses in 1707. Their seat here was demolished in 1833, following neglect after their succession to the dukedom of Atholl and transfer to Blair Castle.

Datestone at Stobhall

Stobhall

Trochrie Castle

WHITEFIELD   NO 089617

The Spalding family had a second seat at Whitefield, close to their other seat of Ashintully, (see page 81). The plan form is the same, a main block 11.2m long by 7.2m wide with a stair wing measuring 5.8m by 5.3m flanking two sides. The main block contained a kitchen and a cellar with its own service stair to the hall above, with a suite of two rooms on top, although the upper parts were mostly dismantled in the early 19th century for materials to build a shepherd's house. It had been altered in the 18th century. There are several gunports in the lowest level.

WILLIAMSTOUN   NO 972220   V

This building is said to have been built c1657 for the heir of the Oliphant laird of Gask after he was disinherited in favour of a younger brother because he married the young daughter of the minister of Trinity-Gask instead of the suitor intended for him, the 45-year old sister of the Marquess of Douglas. The estate had been purchased from William Blair of Kinfauns. The house has a main block of two storeys and an attic. In the middle of one side is a round stair-turret with a square caphouse. The topmost rooms are reached via a turret corbelled out over a re-entrant angle.

OTHER FORMER CASTLES IN PERTHSHIRE

ABERCAIRNY NN913226 Seat of Murrays since 1290s. Modern house in site of castle.
ARDVORLICH NN633229   Site of Stewart castle on southern side of Loch Tay.
AUCHLESHIE NN 654072 Site of castle of the Buchanan family.
BENDOCHTY NO 210455 Wooded mound near modern sand quarries.
BLAIRCESSNOCK NS 617987 A motte lying in Flanders Moss.
BOVAIN NN 541306 Approximate location of MacNab castle to north of River Dochart.
CARGILL NO 157374 Mound 50m across on top of Richard de Montifiquet's castle. p5.
CARNBEDDIE NO 150311 Mound by farm may mark site of King MacBeth's seat.
CASTLETON NN 939240 Site of castle of the earls of Strathearn.
CONDIE NO 076182 A steading with reset stones lies on site of tower or old house.
COLLICHAT NN688038 Part of building, probably a Z-plan, survived until the 1890s.
DUNALASTAIR NN 688074 Site of castle of the Robertson family.
DUNCRUB NO 007157 Site of castle. A Rollo seat since 1380.
DUNFALLANDY NN 949560   House of 1812 on site of castle. Furgusson seat until 1990s.
EILEAN RAN NN 577334 Approx site of MacNab castle burned in the 17th century.
FEDDALL NN 824089 Stewarts' ruined house dated 1683 has later & possiibly older parts.
FINCASTLE NN 870622 Stewart seat. West wing dated 1640. rest of 1702, 1751, etc.
FORTEVIOT NN 616243 Slight mound by church is possible site of early royal palace.
FORTINGALL NN 734466 Ditch 15m wide around platform 30m by 46m in Roman camp.
FOWLIS NN 937240 Earthworks beside ravine. Seat of Stewart earls of Strathearn.
GARTINCABER NN 698001 Possible 17th century walling in 18th century part of house.
GLASSINGALL NN 798045 House on or near site of castle of the Chisholm family.
GLENGYLE NN 385135 Remains of a MacGregor castle still stood in the 19th century.
GREENLOAMING NN 835069 Tree-clad motte called The Roundel to south of A9.
HA TOWER NO 043146 Site of former Graham seat above burn in the Garvock estate.
KEILLOUR NN 979256 19th century house is said to be on site of castle or old house.
KINCARDINE NS 721989 Site of castle of the Drummonds, ruinous by 1714.
MURIE NO 235223 The 6m high Law Knoll is probably a motte.
NEWHALL NO 186319 Castle mentioned in 16th century. Part of it still stood in 1810.
ROTMELL NO 004470 Site of supposedly once-royal castle. Last remains removed 1810
WESTER SHIAN NN842400 Last remains of a castle here were removed in 1820.
Also: Burnbank NS 710988, Fearnan NN725446, Mailer NO 099202 Pubil NN 466423.

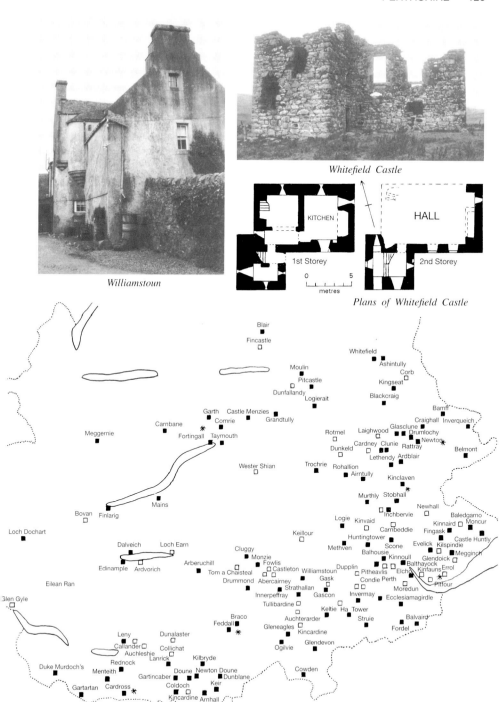

Williamstoun

Whitefield Castle

KITCHEN

1st Storey

HALL

2nd Storey

0 5

metres

Plans of Whitefield Castle

Blair

Fincastle

Whitefield

Moulin

Ashintully

Corb

Pitcastle

Kingseat

Dunfallandy

Logierait

Blackcraig

Garth Castle Menzies

Bamff

Carnbane

Comrie

Grandtully

Craighall Inverqueich

Meggernie

Fortingall Taymouth

Rotmel

Laighwood

Glasclune

Drumlochy

Newton

Cardney Clunie

Rattray

Belmont

Dunkeld

Lethendy Ardblair

Wester Shian

Trochrie

Rohallion

Airntully

Kinclaven

Murthly Stobhall

Newhall

Bovan

Finlarig

Mains

Logie

Kinvaid

Inchbervie

Baledgarno

Loch Dochart

Keillour

Carnbeddie

Kinnaird Moncur

Fingask

Dalveich Loch Earn

Cluggy

Huntingtower

Scone

Evelick Kilspindie

Castle Huntly

Methven

Balhousie

Kinnoull

Glendoick

Megginch

Arberuchill

Monzie

Fowlis

Balthayock

Errol

Edinample Ardvorich

Tom a Chaisteal

Castleton

Williamstoun

Dupplin

Pitheavlis

Elcho

Kinfauns

Eilean Ran

Drummond Abercairney

Gask

Condie Perth

Pitfour

Glen Gyle

Innerpeffray

Strathallan

Gascon

Invermay

Moredun

Tullibardine

Keltie Ha Tower

Ecclesiamagirdle

Braco

Auchterarder

Balvaird

Leny

Feddall

Gleneagles

Kincardine

Struie

Fordel

Callander

Dunalaster

Collichat

Ogilvie

Glendevon

Auchleshie

Lanrick

Kilbryde

Duke Murdoch's

Rednock

Doune Newton Doune

Cowden

Menteith

Gartincaber

Dunblane

Gartartan Cardross

Coldoch

Keir

Kincardine Arnhall

CASTLES OF DUNBARTONSHIRE AND STIRLINGSHIRE

AIRTH   NS 900868   A

An English pele on this dramatic site rising 27m above the Pow Burn and overlooking the Firth of Forth was captured by William Wallace in 1297. Airth then belonged to the family of Airth of that Ilk, but in the early 15th century it passed by marriage to a younger son of a Bruce of Clackmannan. A castle on the site was burned by James III during the conflicts of 1488 that culminated in his murder. James IV sent the laird £100 soon after his accession to help pay for rebuilding. The oldest part of the present building now used as an hotel is a tower house built immediately after this event. It measures 10m by 8.5m and has a staircase in the NE corner, latrines in the SE corner, and a blocked fireplace at hall level in the west wall. In the 16th century a wing the same width and 16m long was added to the west. It contained a hall and private room over two cellars and a kitchen at the east end linked by a passage on the north side. In 1581 another wing was added to the NE and in the eastern re-entrant angle between the two wings is a square tower with a wide spiral staircase and an embattled top with angle-rounds and corbelling. A west wing is shown on an estate plan of 1721, but had gone by the time another was made in 1762. Stones by the stables have initials of the heiress Jean Bruce, who married Sir Thomas Elphinstone in the 1670s. The castle then passed to the Dundas family, but was sold to James Graham, Judge-Admiral of Scotland in 1717. In 1807 whatever then remained of the barmkin wall to the north was swept away and the western angle between the two wings filled with a semi-circular saloon with beyond it a range with a symmetrical facade to the NW with a round tower at each end and a square vaulted entrance hall in the middle.

Airth Castle (see also page 128)

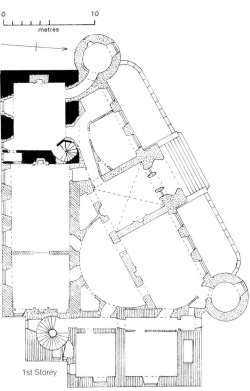

1st Storey

Plan of Airth Castle

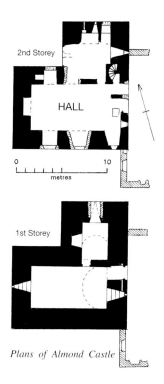

2nd Storey

HALL

0   10
metres

1st Storey

Plans of Almond Castle

Almond Castle

ALMOND   NS 956772   V

This L-plan 15th century tower passed from the Crawfords to the Livingstones in 1540. they added apartments, now very ruined, between the tower and a barmkin wall 1.3m thick lying about 3m away from its north and east sides. No other parts remain of this wall so its full size and shape cannot now be assessed. The original name of Haining was officially changed to Almond in 1633, when the title of Baron Almond was created for the Earl of Linlithgow's son James. The Livingstone earl of Callander lost the castle for his part in the 1715 rebellion. In 1860 the castle was said to have a ditch 16ft wide around it once filled with water from a small stream. The tower has a main block 12.3m long by 8.5m wide with a wing 7.2m wide projecting 4.6m from the north side. There are separate entrances with draw-bar slots to the cellar and hall of the main block in the east end wall beside where the wing adjoins. There was no stair between these levels but there is a hatch in the top of the eastern of two narrow loops lighting the cellar. From the upper entrance a spiral staircase leads up to what was probably a suite of two rooms in the main block, with a third in the wing, and there was a similar arrangement on the fourth storey. At hall level the wing contains a kitchen. The hall windows are mostly later in their present form but the fireplace at the west end is original and some original windows and other features survive in the upper storeys.

ARDINCAPLE   NS 282830

Most of this mansion was demolished in 1957 to make room for a naval housing estate but one square tower of uncertain date is said to survive. It was mostly of c1770, when the Campbells purchased the ruined late 16th century MacAulay castle. Part of the moat was still visible in the 1930s. In the late 19th century it passed to the Colquhouns of Luss.

Airth Castle

ARDMORE   NS 317785

The house was rebuilt in 1654 and enlarged in 1806. Three 16th or 17th century towers or turrets remain, one having gunloops. Ardmore was once the seat of the Geils family.

AUCHENBOWIE   NS 798874

A building contract of 1666 refers to the present L-plan house with an octagonal staircase turret in the re-entrant angle. One pediment is dated 1768. The stone dated 1506 with the Bruce arms is probably 17th or 18th century. In the 1690s Captain William Bruce killed a relative in a duel, and in 1708 the house passed via an heiress to the Monros.

AUCHINVOLE   NS 714769

The 16th century tower house with round bartizans of the Stark family is incorporated into a mansion. One end of the tower has a cross-gable. A kitchen lies in the basement.

BADENHEATH   NS 714724

The last remains of this ashlar-faced 15th century tower were cleared away c1957, leaving only two pediments dated 1661 with initials E.W.K and I.C.K. It measured 12.6m by 9.1m and had a basement divided into two cellars and a lobby which connected the entrance with a spiral staircase in one corner. A secondary stair rose in the corner diagonally opposite. The entrance had an unusal shaped top, perhaps a 16th century alteration. The larger of the two cellars had dumb-bell shaped loops and a square recess in one corner. Part of the hall still remained above, with one jamb of a fine fireplace in an end wall.

BALGLASS   NS 585876

All that remains of the "large dwelling-place or castle, of an antiquated construction" recorded under the name Barons Place in 1795 is a platform measuring 27m by 33m with ruins of 19th century farm buildings on a bluff above the Balglass Burn. At the NE corner the revetment of the platform is as much as 4.5m high, and on the SE corner it is 3m high. John Stirling of Craigbarnet was given a charter of the lands here in 1486. A stone with the date 1602 and the initials of Michael Stirling has been removed to the nearby farmhouse. Balglass later passed to the Bontines, one of whom in 1646 murdered the Reverend Collins, Presbyterian minister of Campsie.

BALLAGAN   NS 572975

A house of 1760, altered in 1896, lies on or near the site of a castle of the Earls of Lennox with two courts and a moat crossed by a drawbridge. Originally known as Campsie, it was renamed Strathblane in 1390, and renamed again as Ballagan in 1425 after the execution of the then earl by James I. From at least 1522 until 1756 it was held by the Stirlings.

BALLINDALLOCH   NS 535885

The Coopers' large 19th century mansion stands on the site of a castle of the earls of Glencairn which passed to the Dunmores in the 18th century. A 17th century sundial survives.

BALLOCH   NS 387526

A moated platform by the south end of Loch Lomond is the site of a manor house from which the Lennox family signed 13th and 14th century charters.

BANNACHRA   NS 343843

The ruined rectangular block 14.2m long by 7.3m wide in a garden may have existed by 1592, when the Mac-Gregors attacked a castle here and shot with an arrow through a window the laird, Sir Humphrey Colquhoun. He was supposedly illuminated by the lamp of a treacherous servant. The Colquhouns had succeeded the Galbraiths at Bannachra in 1512. The east wall containing the fireplace and flue of the kitchen in the basement and a spiral stair has fallen. The entrance was in the south wall beside the stair. The upper windows on the south side have gunloops below their sills.

Half-buried doorway at Bruce's Castle

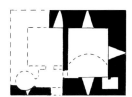

Plan of Badenheath Castle

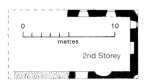

2nd Storey

1st Storey

Plans of Bannachra Castle

Bannachra Castle

The Blair, Blairlogie

Bardowie Castle

Plan of The Blair   *Plan of Bardowie Castle*

BARDOWIE   NS 580739

This tower amongst trees on the north side of Bardowie Loch bears the date 1566 and the initials and arms of John Hamilton and Marion Colquhoun, for whom it was built. A turbulent branch of the Hamiltons of Cadzow (one was killed fighting the Logans of Balvie in 1526, and his successor died fighting the Campbells) were lairds here from the 15th century until the mid 18th century. It then passed via an heiress to Thomas Buchanan of Spittal-Leny, descendants of whom still live in the adjoining mansion dating from the late 17th, 18th and 19th centuries. The tower measures 9.6m by 8.1m and has rounded corners. The south wall is thickened to contain a straight staircase, now blocked, from the entrance near the SW corner to the hall. The cellar has a segmental vault spanning its long axis, an unusual arrangement. The hall retains its vault but no other features apart from a straight stair to the third storey. From the top of this stair in the SE corner rises a spiral stair to the fourth storey (which is mostly within the roof) and onto a section oif wall-walk on the south side. Another section of wall-walk on the north side is reached by its own stair in the NW corner.

BLAIRLOGIE   NS 827948   V

The main block of this building now called The Blair on a shelf above the village has over the dormer windows the date 1543 and initials of its builder Alexander Spittal and his wife Elizabeth Hay. It is a modest structure just 8.5m long by 5.6m wide over walls 0.75m thick containing a hall and bedroom linked by a stair in a round projection at the SE corner, and two vaulted cellars. The bartizan on the SW corner is an addition of the 1580s when Adam Spittal added a NE wing 5.6m wide and 7.4m long containing an extra living room and an attic bedroom above a kitchen. Those windows which are unaltered have holes for three vertical stanchions. The window projecting from the south end and various extensions to the north and east date from after the property passed from the Spittals in the late 18th century.

BOQUHAN   NS 669945

The last remains of this castle of the Grahams were removed c1760. At that time a former yett was still remembered. The site may actually have been to the SW at 661935, on or near where an 18th century two storey house called Auldhall now stands.

BOTURICH   NS 386845

In the 1830s the cellars and other parts of a ruined 15th century castle of the Haldanes overlooking Loch Lomond were incorporated in a large new mansion built by John Buchanan. In the 17th century it had been sacked by the MacFarlanes of Arrochar, and it went to the Buchanans of Ardoch in 1792. It was damaged by fire c1850 and passed to the Findlays.

Bruce's Castle

BRUCE'S   NS 857878

Only the vaulted basement and a fragment of the hall above, including a fireplace at the north end, now remain of an early 15th century tower. It is 16m long by 10m wide over walls 2m thick, except that the southern two thirds of the west wall are thickened to 2.8m by means of an external projection to contain a small mural room and a staircase leading towards the SW corner. The half-buried entrance is in the east side. This building was originally called the Tower of Carnock and formed part of the estate of Sir William de Airth of Plane, who may have been its builder. In 1480 it passed to Alexander Hepburn but in 1489 was wrecked and the yett removed during a family quarrel. The Bruces of Auchenbowie came into possession a few years later and in 1512 Robert Bruce obtained a licence from James IV to refortify and embattle the tower. The crosswalls in the basement (now full of rubble) were probably then inserted. In 1608 the tower was granted to Alexander Drummond but his original residence of Carnock House nearby was declared to be the principal messuage of the barony of Carnock, and from then on the old tower came to be known as Bruce's Castle. See page 129.

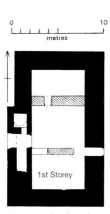

0   10
metres

1st Storey

Bruce's Castle: plan

Boturich Castle

Callendar House

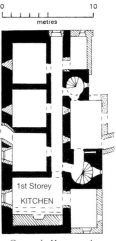

Carnock House: plan

BUCHANAN   NS 457886

The Buchanan family held this estate until it was sold in 1682 to the 3rd Marquess of Montrose, created a duke in 1707, and chief enemy of Rob Roy MacGregor. He replaced the castle by a new house, although old parts may have survived. Further additions were made in 1751 and 1789 but only a fragment survived demolition after a fire in 1850 and the site is now a golf course. A new house was then built further east, itself now a ruin within a housing estate. Within it the Nazi deputy Rudolf Hess was held after flying to Britain in 1942.

CALLENDAR   NS 899793

The Livingstones obtained the estate by marrying a de Callantyr heiress in the 14th century and it remained their principal seat until James, 5th Earl of Linlithgow and 4th Earl of Callendar was forfeited for his part in the 1715 Jacobite rebellion. Their castle was captured by Cromwell and later used as a headquarters by General Monk when he was ruling Scotland. The nucleus of the house is a 14th or 15th century L-plan tower to which an eastern block was added in the 16th century. Another wing was added further east in the 17th century, and by the end of that century the house had assumed its present long narrow shape.

CAMERON   NS 376831   A

This house by Loch Lomond is mostly of 1830 and 1865 but may incorporate parts either of a castle of the Lennox family or the house added to an older tower in the 17th century. The Smolletts bought it in 1763. Johnson and Boswell were entertained here in 1772.

CAMIS ESKAN   NS 321815

In the Campbells' house of 1840 and 1915 is a vaulted basement, either a relic of an old tower of the Dennistouns of Colgrain or of a house built in replacement or alongside of a tower in 1648. In the 20th century it became a TB hospital but is now divided into flats. There may also have been a second old house at Colgrain at 324801 closeby to the SE.

CARBETH   NS 524876

The Buchanans built a castle here after acquiring this former Graham estate in 1476. Most of the existing house, now flats, is of 1840 and 1879, but it may incorporate older parts. From it came a stone dated 1716 with the initials W.B. for one of the Buchanans.

CARNOCK   NS 865882

The house of three storeys and an attic built by Sir Robert Drummond and Margaret Elphinstone lay empty for some years before being demolished by a mining company in 1941. Sir Robert was Master of Works to James VI in the 1570s. There were rooms at either end of a central hall and further private rooms were provided in a pair of matching wings on the south side. Parts of it, especially the fine plaster ceilings, were the work of the Nicolsons, who obtained Carnock in 1634 and became baronets in 1637. The house passed to the Shaws of Greenock in the early 18th century.

CASTLE CARY   NS 786775

This tower on a narrow ridge above the Red Burn was built in the 1480s by Henry Livingstone to replace an earlier structure on the site. It measures 10.2m by 6.9m and rises through a vaulted cellar and three upper storeys to a parapet, the top of which is 12.7m above the ground, and which surrounds an attic. The staircase in the NW corner projects within the rooms and small chambers have been divided off them at this end. The entrance lies at the foot of this stair. There are latrines in trhe NW corner. An east wing of two storeys and an attic is probably 18th century, but over the doorway into the base of a stair turret set against the junction of the two parts is a stone with the date 1679. There are indications of a wing having stood against the western half of the north wall of the tower. There was latterly a length of barmkin walling here which has been removed since the 1880s. Since then a yett once in the doorway of the stair-turret has been transferred to the doorway connecting the basements of the two parts. Castle Cary was held by the Livingstones of Dunipace in the 16th and 17th centuries but by the 1690s had passed to the Baillies, who were descended from the Baliol family. The castle was burnt by a party of Highlanders in the Jacobite rebellion of 1715. Thomas Dundas of Fingask married the heiress Bethia Baillie in 1730.

CASTLE RANKINE   NS 785818

There is now nothing left to see of this castle west of the farmhouse on the east side of the ravine of the burn. Excavations in 1938-9 found traces of a wall 1.1m to 1.4m thick around a court 29m from north to south by 27.5m from east to west. From the north wall a barbican extended across a berm 8m wide to the edge of a ditch 6m wide around the three sides not naturally defended. Architectural fragments discovered suggested a date late in the 13th century and it has been suggested that this is the site of the place of Gertranky, mentioned in a writ of Edward I of England dated 1299, and then belonging to Sir Herbert de Morham. Potsherds of the 14th to the 16th century indicated the site long remained occupied.

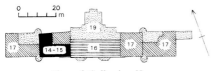

Plan of Callendar House

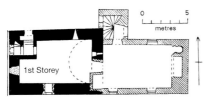

Plan of Castle Cary

Castle Cary

CATTER   NS 473871

The earls of Lennox had a castle here on a motte by a ford on Endrick Water. Inchmurrin Castle may have superseded it. The classical style house built by the Dukes of Montrose to the west in 1767 probably replaced the manor house at Catter mentioned in 1505.

COLZIUM   NS 729788

A 5m high and 14.6m length of walling, with evidence of vaulting over a kitchen with a fire-place and an adjoining cellar with a gunloop, is all that remains of the castle of the Livingstones of Kilsyth. A stone dated 1575 is said to have been removed from the ruin. The castle is thought to have been demolished in 1703 and the new mansion of Colzium House was built by the Edmonstones of Duntreath somewhat later.

CRAIGIEVERN   NS 495902

On a rise above a stream draining into the Altquhur are scanty traces of a court about 23m across within a wall up to 3m thick. This suggests a structure similar to Loch Doon Castle in Ayrshire dating from the late 13th or early 14th century. The Buchanans later held the estate. Nearby is a three storey T-plan house of the mid to late 18th century.

CRAIGMADDIE   NS 575765

This ruin within a hill-fort east of Craigmaddie House was probably built c1480-1520. Until they moved to Bardowie in the 1560s this was a seat of a branch of the Hamiltons, who obtained the estate in the early 15th century, the previous owners having been the Galbraiths of Baldernock. The tower measures 8.4m by 7.4m over walls 1.5m thick. The vaulted basement buried in rubble has just a loop at each end and a hatch to the hall above where an entrance lay in the SE wall. This level is very ruined but has signs of a window in each sidewall at the other end, a stair in the east wall to lost upper levels, and an aumbry beside the doorway.

CULCREUGH   NS 620876

Andrew Galbraith is mentioned as laird of Culcreugh in a document of 1472, but the existing tower is probably a generation more recent than that. It measures 12.3m by 8.5m over walls 1.6m thick and rises 12.7m to the top of the parapet surrounding an attic. Below are a pair of cellars, a hall, and a third storey probably always divided into two rooms as it is now. In 1630 Robert Galbraith sold the estate to Alexander Seton of Gargunnock. He in turn disposed of the lands in 1632 to Robert Napier, a younger son of John Napier of Merchiston. The initials of a later John Napier and his wife Margaret Lennox with the date 1721 appear over the south doorway of a four storey wing added to the middle of the east side, although the wing itself may be later and was probably built by Peter Spiers of Elderslie, who acquired the castle in 1769. His descendants owned it until 1890. Embedded in still later additions on the north side is a staircase of about the same period which now connects the tower rooms, and the original narrow stair projecting into the rooms has been removed. The windows of the tower are also mostly of the 18th century except for four loops in the cellars, three of them now blocked. Culcreugh supposedly held a Cromwellian ngarrison in the 1650s.

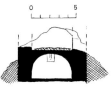

Culcreugh: plan   *Craigmaddie: plans and section*

DARLEITH   NS 346806

Embedded in the north side of a large later ruined mansion by a burn is a small and much-altered tower of c1600 built by the Darleith family. It has walls up to 1.4m thick and a tiny round bartizan on one corner

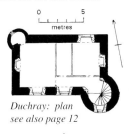

*Duchray: plan
see also page 12*

Culcreugh Castle

Duchray Castle

DUCHRAY   NS 480998

This castle was built either by John Graham of Downance, to whom Duchray was sold in 1569 by John Drummond, or his son William. Here in 1653 the Earl of Glencairn raised the Royalist force that defeated the Cromwellians at Aberfoyle, the then laird, another John, taking an active part in the campaign. In the 1690s two Graham sisters entertained dragoon officers of William III's army at the front door whilst Rob Roy MacGregor was smuggled out at the back. The castle consists of a three storey main block measuring 10.7m by 6.2m over walls 1m thick with a round stair turret at the SE corner and a round bartizan at the top of the NW corner. The windows, doorways and fireplaces all appear to be of c1825, when the castle was restored from ruin.

Darleith

DUMBARTON   NS 400745   HS

The prominent volcanic crag overlooking the Clyde is a natural site for a fortress and was used in the Dark Ages as the seat of the kingdom of Strathclyde, being mentioned in a mid 5th century letter of St Patrick. It was besieged and captured by a combined force of Picts and Northumbrians in 756, it was sacked again in 780, and in 870 was captured when the well dried up after a four month siege by Vikings from Ireland. There are no remains of this period, during which the eastern rock, The Beak, is thought to have borne the buildings of a town, whilst the western crag was occupied by the royal palace-citadel.

After Scotland was united as one kingdom Dumbarton remained a royal stronghold. Not much is known about it for much of the medieval period, although it is mentioned in 1238 in a charter to the Earl of Lennox, when the castle was reserved to the Crown, and in 1333 David II and his consort Joan took refuge in the castle after the English victory at Halidon Hill. The Portcullis Arch dates from about that time. In the 1390s Walter de Danyelstone seized the castle and only gave it up in exchange for the bishopric of St Andrews. Patrick Galbraith occupied the castle in 1443. He was ejected by the deputy governor, Sir Robert Sempill, who was killed when Galbraith returned with a large force. In 1489 Lord Darnley, son of the Earl of Lennox, held the castle against James IV. A siege was raised after much of the town was burnt by the garrison in a sally, but a subsequent siege proved more sucessful. James IV used Dumbarton as a naval base and set out from here on his expeditions to pacify the Western Isles. In adulthood James V used Dumbarton for the same purpose, although during his minority the castle was captured by the Earl of Lennox and the Master of Glencairn, whose forces tunnelled under the weak north gate, and was then held against the regent.

Entrance to Dumbarton Castle

The Earl of Lennox was again in possession in 1542. On behalf of the English Crown he seized French supplies and funds landed at Dumbarton which were intended to aid the Regent Arran. The regent besieged and captured the castle, and in 1548 the young Queen Mary stayed here after the defeat at Pinkie until she was taken to France to marry the Dauphin. After Mary's abdication the castle continued to be held in her interest by Lord Fleming. It was besieged by the Regent Moray in January 1570 but a French fleet arrived and the attack was abandoned after Moray's murder in Linlithgow. On 1st April 1571 the castle was captured by Captain Thomas Crawfurd of Jordanhill and a party of 100 men who scaled the rock on the sheerest NE side with the aid of ropes and ladders. Lord Fleming escaped but John Hamilton, Archbishop of St Andrews was captured and executed. In 1581 the former regent the Earl of Morton was incarcerated in the castle, and in 1614 Patrick Stewart, Earl of Orkney was held prisoner within it. In March 1639 a party of Covenanters captured the castle governor at church and forced him to surrender the castle, then in a delapidated state. In 1652 it was surrendered without a siege to the Cromwellian Major-General Lambert. The defences were still neglected and in 1654 some Royalists made a successful surprise raid. New defences were built in the late 17th and early 18th centuries. The army abandoned the site as obsolete in 1865, only to re-occupy it during each of the two world wars.

The castle does not have a continuous set of walls since the rock was considered sheer enough for parts of the circuit. The highest part of the rock bears the foundations of the White Tower, a structure 7m in diameter of uncertain date, but too small and weak to be a 13th century keep. The much larger and lower eastern summit carries a magazine built in the 1740s. Various domestic and storage buildings in this vicinity which are shown as still roofed in Slezer's view of 1693 were then cleared away. There is a sentry box on the walls here and nearby is the Prince of Wales Battery of c1790 on the site of a half-round battery of c1575. Between the two summits is a cleft which provided access. On the north side there was a curtain wall with a simple archway until the five storey Wallace Tower, of which just the basement now survives, was built in 1617. The remains were incorporated in the Duke of York Battery of 1795 in which stood a barrack-block, now demolished. Nearby is a building of the 1730s called the French Prison because of its usage during the Napoleonic Wars.

The southern approach has a more complex series of defences. At the foot is a gateway beside the King George Battery of the 1730s. On the salient angle of the battery is a pepperpot-shaped sentry box on bold cornelling. Within the battery stands the Governor's House of the 1730s on the side of a medieval gatehouse block 23m long by 8m deep. Steps then lead firstly to the Guard House, a 16th century building remodelled c1730, and then to the lofty pointed Portcullis Arch, the only medieval standing relic, which in later years had a gunnery store built upon it. The original portcullis was later superseded by a heavy hinged gate.

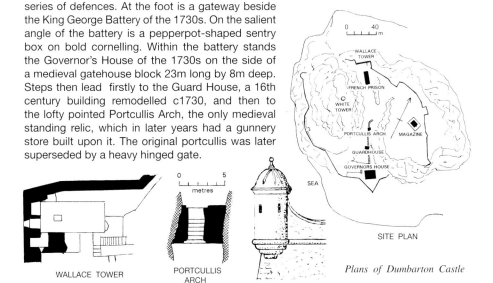

WALLACE TOWER

PORTCULLIS ARCH

SEA

SITE PLAN

Plans of Dumbarton Castle

DUNGLASS   NS 435735   V

On a rocky headland projecting into the north side of the Clyde, within the secure compound of a former oil refinery, is the former seat of the Colquhouns, who acquired what was probably an already existing castle here in 1439. On the south side is the outer wall of a range which contained apartments over cellars, the upper rooms having windows with seats in the embrasures. Sections of the parapet corbelling still remain. This block may date from the 1470s, when Sir John Colquhoun was Chamberlain of Scotland under James III. The castle is said to have been fortified by James IV during his siege of Dumbarton Castle in 1489. In the NW corner is a three storey house lying from north to south and having a bartizan on the outermost corner. This part, recently re-roofed to preserve it, and still occupied until the 1920s, after which it became a stationary store, was probably the work of Humphrey Colquhoun, who was treacherously slain at Bannachra in 1592. The wall containing the entrance arch on the north appears to be of the same period as the adjacent house, and the thin and low walls and the dovecot on the east side of the court measuring about 45m across are also likely to be of that period. The NE corner rises to a knob of rock bearing a monument of 1836 to Provost Henry Bell. It is likely a 14th or 15th century tower once stood here.

Dunglass Castle

In the conflicts of the 1630s the castle was garrisoned with an ensign, a sergeant and thirty men. It decayed during the 18th century, when parts were demolished to provide stone for building nearby quays. The castle was purchased by Alexander Buchanan of Auchentorlie in 1812, and in the 1830s the house was remodelled and given a west wing, whilst further work was done in the 1850s, when the circular SW turret was added. Dunglass was sold in 1899 to the Macdonalds, one of whose daughters was married to the architect Charles Rennie Mackintosh. Little survives of the new interiors he designed for the house in 1900, and a valuable fireplace and mantlepiece have recently been removed.

Dunglass Castle

Dunglass Castle

Dunmore Tower

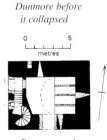

Dunmore before it collapsed

0 5
metres

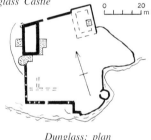

Dunglass: plan

Dunglass Castle (see also page 158

Dunmore: plan

DUNMORE NS 890889

A barony of Elphinstone was created in 1504 for Sir John Elphinstone and the tower was then built as its main seat. John, 4th Earl of Dunmore purchased the estate in 1754 and in 1759 renamed the tower Dunmore. A new mansion called Dunmore Park was erected by the 5th Earl in the 1820s and the old tower was then provided with a new parapet and top turret to serve as a folly or eye-catcher, and at the same time converted into the family burial-place, coffins being stored in the vaulted basement, where the two loops were blocked up and a new north-facing doorway inserted. The tower measures 8.9m by 7.2m over walls mostly about 1.7m thick. Since the 1960s the western half of the three upper storeys has collapsed, the rubble and fallen fragments still being as they fell. Bones and coffins are scattered around since the burial place is currently open. Most of the upper features currently visible are 19th century but a triangular moulded pediment (now fallen) on the north side indicated that some remodelling took place in the 17th century.

DUNTREATH   NS 536810

In the 1360s Donald, Earl of Lennox granted Duntreath to his brother Murdoch. James I executed Earl Duncan in 1425 and gave the estate to William Edmonstone of Culloden, who had married the king's sister Mary. The lands have belonged to the Edmonstones ever since and were made into a barony by James II in 1452. A tower containing two rooms on each of two upper storeys over a pair of vaulted cellars was then built against the NW end of a late 14th century range probably originally serving as a hall-block, but made into a chapel in the 16th century. Measuring 14.5m by 8m over walls 1.4m thick, the tower is now the only part of the ancient buildings to survive and has been much altered over the years. It is entered through a small projection containing a staircase on the SW side. A second stair in the north corner also serves each storey and has beside it a latrine corbelled out at second storey level. There is another latrine of this type projecting at third storey level at the far end of the NE side.

At the turn of the 16th and 17th centuries Sir James Edmonstone built ranges on the SE and SW sides of a court with a high tower in the re-entrant angle containing a scale-and-platt staircase. It was named the "Dumb Laird's Tower" from the late 17th century occupant of the room over the top of the staircase. A lengthy description of the walls to be harled by John McWilliams under a contract of 1631 with Sir Archibald Edmonstone mentions not only the fine inner gatehouse, a block 9m by 6m with a vaulted passage between guard-rooms with gunports in the middle of the screen wall closing off the NW side of the court, but an outer gatehouse as well. The castle fell into ruin in the 18th century when the family resided in Ireland, but between 1857 and 1871 the 13th laird and 3rd baronet, Sir Archibald, restored the building and used it again as the family seat. A large new mansion was then built on the side of the SW range, a new gatehouse built, and the surviving old parts remodelled. In 1958 the building was reduced to its present size, leaving the 15th century tower isolated on the lawn in front of the present house.

Duntreath Castle

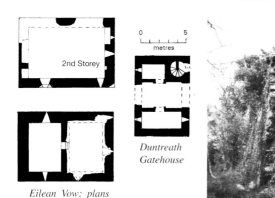

2nd Storey

0   5
metres

*Duntreath
Gatehouse*

Eilean Vow: plans

Eilean Vow Castle

EILEAN VOW   NS 332128

At the south end of a small tree-clad island is a ruined and ivy-mantled tower built by the MacFarlanes in the 16th century. A stair in the NE corner connected the main room with two vaulted cellars below, one of them now choked with rubble. The stair to the third storey must have been in the NW corner, which is destroyed at that level. The SE corner seems to have contained a stair from the third storey to the attic. The ruin shows signs of 18th century repairs in the form of renewed quoins and a renewed window on the south side at second storey level, but it was ruined by 1814, when the poet William Wordsworth found a hermit living in the surviving vault.

FINTRY   NS 641863

On a commanding knoll are low featureless fragments of a tower about 8.4m wide and over 14m long over walls 1.8m thick. It was probably built by Sir Robert Graham, whose nephew Patrick, Lord Graham gave him an estate here in 1460. The castle was a ruin by 1724. Building stone for the castle was taken from a quarry or ditch immediately to the south.

GARDEN   NS 593948

Nothing now remains of this tower. It was a ruin by 1724 and was demolished by 1749, although parts of it still survived until the mid 19th century, being then surrounded by a rampart and ditch described as "pretty entire". It belonged to the Stirlings of Keir. Rob Roy is said to have once occupied the castle in the laird's absence and held it against him until payment was received.

Last remains of Fintry Castle

GARGUNNOCK   NS 717948 & 715944

Nothing now remains of the homestead moat here. Blind Harry's account of the adventures of William Wallace, probably written in the late 15th century, describes an attack on "a small peill" here containing an English garrison and having "within a dyk, bathe closs, chawmer, and hall". The ditch was crossed by a drawbridge.

Embedded in the middle of Gargunhnock House is a much-altered L-plan house built by one of the Setons of Touch, who held the estate from the early 16th century until it was granted to the Earl of Mar in 1624. It was probably he who lengthened the main block by one compartment and built a wing west of it, thus making a Z-shaped plan. In the late 17th century the house was purchased by James Campbell, Writer to the Signet. Later the estate passed by marriage firstly to the Campbells of Ardkinglass and then to the Livingstones of Glentirran. They added a NW wing and demolished the barmkin wall and gateway, whilst a SE wing and a staircase between it and the original NE wing of the oldest part were added by Colonel James Eldingtoun shortly after he acquired Gargunnock in 1793. Futher alterations were carried out by bthe Stirlings, who have been at Gargunnock since they purchased it in 1835.

GARTNESS   NS 502865

Only a mound survives to mark the site of this castle by Endrick Water. It was a Napier seat from 1495. There was once a stone from it dated 1574 at Gartness Mill.

GEILSTON   NS 339783   NTS

The Scottish National Trust opens to the public the grounds and walled garden of this two storey harled house, which is probably 17th century but with newer and possibly older parts. The Woods family are thought to have once had a tower here.

GLORAT   NS 641779 & 644786

The Stirling family have been at Glorat since 1508, and in 1666 Sir George Stirling was made a baronet for his services during the Civil War. Most of the present mansion is of 1869 and 1879 but on the west side is an older nucleus dated 1625 with initials of Mungo Stirling, who succeeded his father as laird in 1642. High above the house is the motte and bailey site of Maiden Castle. A complex of damaged earthworks represents the bailey on the north side of a motte overlooking a drop to the east.

Ditch at Graham's Castle   *Plan of Graham's Castle*

GRAHAM'S   NS 681859   F

This site lies in a clearing in a forest above the Carron Valley Reservoir. On the end of a gentle-sided promontory is a platform 24m square surrounded by a dry moat 10m wide and 3m deep. It is thought to have been the residence of Sir John Graham, who was killed fighting alongside William Wallace at Falkirk in 1298. The thin fragments of masonry to the east are of a later house and court of the Grahams.

HERBERTSHIRE   NS 804830

MacGibbon and Ross describe a lofty turreted L-plan building of some size with many lower later additions which has been demolished. In later years it housed a school. The tower lay above the River Carron and measured 13m by 19m over the longest sides. It was built by the Sinclairs of Rosslyn and passed in 1608 to Alexander Elphinstone, 1st Earl of Linlithgow. In the mid 17th century it went to the Stirlings, by whom in 1768 it was sold to william Morehead. His plans for rebuilding the house were never carried out.

INCH GALBRAITH   NS 369904

This castle occupying all of a tiny island (most likely a crannog) in Loch Lomond was a seat of the Galbraith family. It seems to have had an outer wall about 1.5m thick enclosing a court about 15m by 13m in which were two or three tenement blocks, a layout similar to 15th century Castle Lachlan in Argyll. On the east side is a jamb of a gateway into the tiny central court. The jamb has a portcullis groove. The outer wall still stands two storeys high on the north side, with remains of two upper windows. Of the internal walls the lower part remains of the north wall of the south tenement, with one narrow loop and a jamb of a doorway.

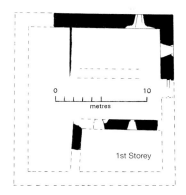

Plan of Inch Galbraith Castle

Graham's Castle

Inch Galbraith Castle

INCH MURRIN   NS 373863

A rocky eminence at the west end of the largest of the many islands in Loch Lomond bears fragments of what appears to be a 14th century tower or hall-house 10.2m wide. The building was probably about 16m long originally but seems to have later been subdivided and an addition made to the east end, whilst a round tower of which little now remains was added to the NW corner. One high fragment remains of each long wall with traces of two basement loops and an upper window on the north side, and a blocked upper window on the south side. After his execution by James I in 1425 the Earl of Lennox's widow retired to live on Inch Murrin until her death in 1460. The castle was the scene of the murder of Sir John Colquhoun in 1439. James IV stayed at the castle in 1506.

INVERSNAID   NN 349096   V

The buidings of Garrison Farm incorporate parts of the 0.7m thick outer walls of a barracks built in 1718-19, wrecked by the Jacobites in 1745, but repaired and kept up for another half century. Nothing survives of the west side which contained the entrance, or of the SW flanker, but footings remain of the NE flanker, with an oven in the outer corner. The walls enclosed a court 18m by 19.5m within which were a pair of three storey barrack blocks on the north and south. On the other sides stairs led up to platforms set over vaulted casemates.

INVERUGLAS   NS 332128

This ruined MacFarlane castle on an island in Loch Lomond is said to have been linked by a causeway to the nearby western shore. It has a main block measuring 12.5m long by 10.5m wide with walling up to 2.2m thick at basement level but much thinner above. This suggests a remodelling c1570-1600 of a tower originally built c1500. The tiny square basement loops are, however, identical to those appearing in the round towers of 5.4m and 3.8m diameter added to two diagonally opposite corners, and they are not obviously later insertions. The smaller tower contains rectangular rooms and starts at a higher level because of the lie of the ground. A barn on the shore nearby has reused bottom roundels of keyhole-shaped loops typical of c1500 which may have come from the castle, or from a vanished former castle at Tighvechtichian, near Tarbert further south.

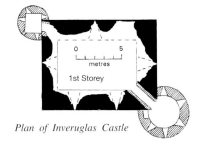

Plan of Inveruglas Castle

Inveruglas Castle

Inch Murrin Castle

KERSIE   NS 871910

This 17th century laird's house with a square turret containing a scale-and-platt staircase in the re-entrant angle was probably built by the Monteith family. It has three storeys and an attic and appears as a mansion with a park on a map of 1654. Now a farmhouse, it may incorporate part of an earlier tower. It passed to the Livingstones, then to the Hopes. It was sold to the Dundas family in 1794 and again in 1892 to the Earl of Ronaldsay.

KILMAHEW   NS 352787

A ruined L-plan castle of the Napiers lies close to a modern mansion built by James Burns, who had purchased the estate in 1859. The main block measures 14.2m by 7.7m and has been much altered, but the entrance retains a drawbar slot. The walls are thin and there are traces of a huge flue at one end, suggesting that originally crosswalls divided the basement into a kitchen and two cellars, a plan form common c1560-1600. However the block rises four storeys to corbelling for a parapet, so the outer shell may be rather earlier.

KILMARONOCK or MAINS   NS 446877

This 15th century tower of the Dennistouns had mullion-and-transom windows and a splayed plinth, both rare features in Scottish towers. Above the plinth it measures 12.2m by 9.8m and was entered on the south side at the level of a vaulted hall on the third of four storeys. This room had a screens passage at the east end with a musicians gallery above reached by a spiral stair in the NE corner. In the SE corner there was a service stair down to the kitchen below, where there was probably a second entrance. The vaulted cellar was reached by a continuation of this stair and also by a second service stair in the west wall. This level was subdivided and had three loops, one now broken out to make a lower entrance. The fourth storey has chambers set either side of a flue in the west wall from the hall fireplace. Another small chamber probably lay in the SE corner. The castle was later held by the Cunninghame earls of Glencairn and then passed to the Cochrane family. See p146.

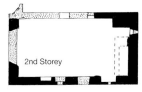

Plans of Kilmahew Castle

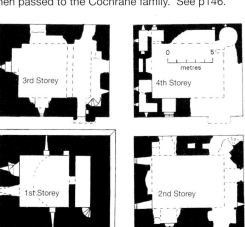

Plans of Kilmaronock Castle

Kilmahew Castle

Kilmaronock or Mains Castle

Mugdock Castle

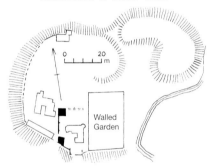

Walled Garden

KILSYTH   NS 720775

There are no remains of the 15th century castle captured by Cromwell in 1650. It belonged to a branch of the Livingstone earls of Linlithgow. In 1661 Sir James Livingstone was made Viscount Kilsyth and Baron Campsie by Charles II, but the honours and estates were lost on the attainder of the 3rd Viscount after the 1715 rebellion.

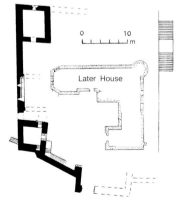

Later House

Plans of Mugdock Castle

MANOR   NS 827948

Little now remains of a T-plan building formerly dated 1572 with initials of Robert Callander, although it stood entire in 1850. The main block was 15m long by 5.4m wide. The wing was short and had a turret stair corbelled out on one side.

MUGDOCK   NS 549772   F

The Grahams held this estate, now a country park, by the mid 13th century. In the late 14th century they built a castle on a platform west of a loch which became the seat of a barony created in 1458. In the late 15th century a large outer court was created to the west and north. In 1644 the castle was raided by the laird of Buchanan on the orders of the Commitee of estates, all munitions being removed along with "all the gaites and iron windows". Mugdock was granted to the Marquess of Argyll after the forfeiture of James Graham, 1st Marquess of Montrose in 1645. Montrose himself was executed in Edinburgh in 1650 after being betrayed by Neil MacLeod of Assynt, but Mugdock was returned to the 2nd Marquis of Montrose in 1655, and he resided in a new house in the middle of the court. This house was replaced in 1875 by a new house built by John Guthrie Smith, now itself very ruinous.

The inner court seems to have been roughly a square of 33m within walls 1.4m thick, although the exact layout of the eastern portion of it is entirely unknown. On the south side was a gatehouse with a frontage 12m long but its width and height are unknown. The passageway led through the western end of the building and was closed by a portcullis. The two towers now surviving within the NW and SW corners are about 8m and 6.7m square respectively, although both are rather irregularly laid out. Little survives of the NW tower other than its vaulted basement. The other tower, recently restored, has a second storey doorway reached by a forestair alongside the curtain wall linking it with the gatehouse. From the entrance a stair in the SE corner leads to the third storey, at which level the walls are corbelled out on three sides to increase the size of upper half of the tower. Straight stairs in the east wall then serve the fourth storey and battlements. The curtain wall between the towers is intact and has gateway at the south end and two loops which served a building to the north which seems to have been remodelled in the 17th century.

The outer court enclosed a space over 100m across from north to south and probably a similar distance the other way, the west and NE sections of walling having gone. On the north one small section of walling remains with a square tower adjoining a ruinous 16th century chapel. On the south side is a 36m long section of walling 6m high and 1.1m thick with keyhole-shaped gunloops and a gateway. The long 16th century range of offices beside this wall remained roofed until c1960.

Mugdock Castle

Old Leckie

OLD LECKIE   NS 690946

The Leckies recovered this estate in 1535, having lost it in the early 15th century, and about a generation or two later they built an L-plan tower. The main block was later extended to the west to make a T-plan, the walls here being slightly thinner. In 1659 it was acquired by David Moir of Craigarnhall, whose descendants remained in possession until the 20th century. The tower is of three storeys with an attic. The entrance in the base of the wing is protected by a machicolation high above, and covered by a gunloop and spyhole. See page 12,

OLD SAUCHIE   NS 779883

The estate then known as Little Sauchie was granted in 1528 to James Erskine, son of Robert, 4th Lord Erskine. The recently restored L-plan tower set above the ravine of the Sauchie Burn dates from c1560 - 1600. It has a main block 11m long by 6.7m wide which contained two vaulted cellars, a hall above, and a third storey possibly divided into two rooms, with closets in round bartizans on the north and east corners. There are gunloops in the bartizans and double-splayed gunports in the cellars. A wing 4.7m wide contained a scale-and-platt staircase to the hall and a bedroom above, upper access being by a turret stair with more gunloops which is corbelled out not over the re-entrant angle as usual but from the outer SE wall. There were attic rooms in the roofs of the main block and wing. In the early 17th century a wing containing a private room over a kitchen was added at the NW end, and in the late 17th or early 18th century a long new wing was extended beyond that. These later parts remain in use. The castle was acquired in 1659 by Alexander Glass of Cultinhove. A century later it passed to David Cheap, and in 1786 was sold to William Ramsey of Barnton.

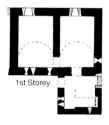

1st Storey

2nd Storey

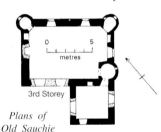

0   5
metres

3rd Storey

Plans of
Old Sauchie

Old Sauchie before restoration

PEEL OF CLAGGANS   NS 521966

Near Borland house and Kelty Water is a ditched D-shaped platform from which foundations of a building were removed in the 19th century.

Plane Castle before restoration

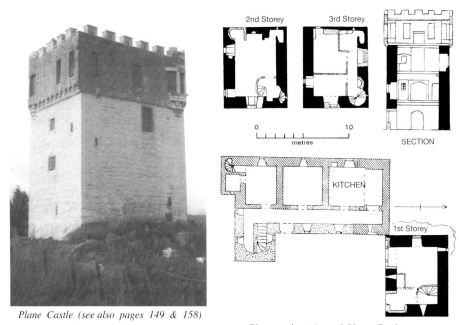

2nd Storey   3rd Storey

0   10
metres

SECTION

KITCHEN

1st Storey

Plane Castle (see also pages 149 & 158)

Plans and section of Plane Castle

PLANE   NS 849869   V

A barony of Plane was created for the d'Erth (Airth) family in 1314. The tower on an outcrop of rock was probably built by Thomas, younger brother of William, 1st Lord Somerville, who obtained the barony in 1449 on his marriage to the heiress Elizabeth d'Erth. In 1634 Plane was purchased from James Somerville by Thomas Nicholson, who is thought to have dismantled the hall range to provide materials for alterations at his house at Carnock. It later passed to the Elphinstones and then to the earls of Dunmore. None of these later owners lived at Plane, which became a farm and fell into ruin. The tower measures 8.3m by 6.8m over walls up to 1.4m thick. The basement was originally vaulted and was entered by a round-arched doorway in the west wall, the only communication with the hall being via a hatch (a stair has now been provided). The hall has its own separate doorway near the SE corner, two windows with seats in the embrasures, a fireplace in the west wall, and a latrine in the NW corner. A spiral stair in the NE corner led to the bedroom above, now divided into two rooms. The other corners all had angle-rounds at parapet level. In c1900 the tower was restored and a fourth storey added. By the 1950s the tower was again roofless but in the 1990s it was purchased and restored by the Wright family. Just touching the tower by one corner now spanned at third storey level by a wooden balcony, is a range of the 1525-30 containing a passage connecting two vaulted cellars and a kitchen at the north end. The upper storeys containing a hall and chamber end-to-end and several bedrooms are entirely restoration work of the 1990s, as is the entrance on the east side and the whole of the staircase wing adjoining it. There is a service stair in second projection at the SW corner.

ROSNEATH   NS 272823

The Marquess of Argyll's house of c1630 just inland from the south end of the bay was wrecked by a fire in 1802. The ruin was demolished to make way for a caravan site in the 1950s. The original castle of the Lennox family here lay on the end of the headland.

ROSSDHU   NS 361896

Only one wall containing the entrance still stands of the tower built by the Colquhouns of Luss c1600 beside Loch Lomond, the rest having been demolished in 1770 to provide the materials for a new house. John Colquhoun was present at the siege of Dumbarton in 1478, and in 1602 Sir James Colquhoun led his kinsmen to a defeat in a clan battle with the MacGregors in Glenfroon.

SKAITHMUIR   NS 888834

In the 19th century this tower measuring 10.4m from east to west by 7.6m wide was much altered to accommodate a pumping engine for a coal-pit. It was demolished in the 1960s after being a gaunt ruined shell for many years. No trace of any staircase linking what were originally four storeys then survived. A window in the west side beside the hall fireplace had the date 1607 and initials of Alexander, 4th Lord Elphinstone, and his wife Dame Jane Livingstone, daughter of William 6th Lord Livingstone.

Rossdhu Castle

STENHOUSE   NS 879829

Reset on the south side of the house was a dormer pediment dated 1622 with initials of its builders, William Bruce and his second wife Rachel Johnston. William obtained the estate from his father in 1611 and was created a baronet of Nova Scotia in 1628. A stone on the north gable dated 1655 had initials and arms of the 2nd baronet, another William, and his wife Helen Douglas of Cavers. On the east side was a stone with the year 1710 and arms and initials of Sir William Bruce, 4th baronet, and his wife Dame Margaret Boyd. The house was a much altered and extended L-plan building of four storeys plus attics, the rooms originally all being connected by a spiral stair in a round turret in the re-entrant angle. This turret survived until the house was demolished c1970, but no longer contained a staircase. The corners had closets in round bartizans and on the outer corner of the L was a rectangular bartizan. There was originally another bartizan on the NW corner of the main block, which measured 11m by 7.3. The wing 6.6m wide projected 6.2m to the north. A housing estate now lies on the site.

STEUARTHALL   NS 828929

Until demolished in the 1980s this L-plan building with a round stair turret in the re-entrant angle and a kitchen in the base of the wing had a stone with the motto "Gang Forward", the date 1703, and initials of Sir Alexander Stirling of Garden and Anna Hamilton, who married in 1686. It was formerly called West Polmaise. Most of the building only had two storeys and an attic and was of the date upon it, or not much earlier, but the four storey west end may have originally been a freestanding tower of measuring 5.7m by 5.4m. built c1600 by the Murrays of Touchadam, but sold soon afterwards to the Cowans. There was a north wing of 1824.

STIRLING   NS 790940   HS

The volcanic rock was probably occupied from early times and is likely to have originally been defended by low but thick drystone walls following the naturally defensible contours of the site. It is first mentioned in connection with Alexander I, who died in his castle at Stirling in 1124. He had built a chapel within the defences a few years previously. His successor David I frequently stayed at Stirling and founded the nearby abbey of Cambuskenneth in 1147. Under the Treaty of Falaise of 1174 Stirling was one of several castles ordered to be surrendered to the English, a consequence of William the Lion's capture at Alnwick in 1173, and part of the process by which Henry I of England attempted to establish an English over-lordship of Scotland. King William died in the castle in 1214 and it may well have been him who first provided a stone curtain wall around a fairly modest area corresponding roughly to the present upper close. There are no actual remains of walls, ditches or buildings of this period, and little is known about the nature of the defences during the Wars of Independence, although the rebuilding recorded in 1287 was with stone and lime.

In 1296 Stirling Castle was given up to Edward I of England, the garrison being demoralised by his slaughter of the defenders of Berwick. William Wallace led the Scots to victory at a battle by Stirling Bridge in 1297, the castle being surrendered to him and dismantled. King Edward had it repaired in 1298 but the Scots recaptured it after the English barons declined to march north to relieve it. Sir William Oliphant held out against the English king during a three month siege in 1304. Local churches were stripped of their lead roofs to weight the siege-engines employed against the castle. Edward insisted on his new engine the War-Wolf being tried against the defences, even though Oliphant had surrendered before the weapon could be commissioned.

Stirling Castle

In 1313 Stirling was blockaded by Edward Bruce, brother of King Robert I, and the governor Sir Philip Mowbray agreed to surrender if relief did not arrive by June 1314. On the agreed day the Scots defeated a much larger English force led by King Edward II whilst it attempted to cross a stream at Bannockburn, and the castle was then duly given up. The defences were dismantled but were restored under Sir Thomas Rokeby after the Scottish defeat at Hamildon Hill. We know that the defences were then of mortared stone although the hall and chambers (and presumably other more humble buildings) were of wood. Edward III relieved the castle during an attack by Sir Andrew Moray in 1337 but it was finally taken back by the Scots in 1342. Robert II appointed his son Robert, Earl of Menteith and Fife, later Duke of Albany, as keeper of the castle, and it was rebuilt and again used as a royal residence. Dating from this period is the oldest part now standing, a gateway passage leading north from the main ward of the castle to the lower ward. It now forms part of a later tower known as The Mint from the one-time use of the upper room.

In 1452 the castle was the scene of the murder of William, 8th Earl of Douglas by James II after the earl was invited under a letter of safe conduct to dinner to discuss differences. During the course of an argument over alleged treasonable activities by the earl he was stabbed by the king and finished off by courtiers. James III was born in the castle in 1451 and was defeated and murdered nearby at Sauchieburn in 1488 after being refused admission by its governor Shaw of Sauchie, who had turned the king's heir over to the rebels. The terraced garden known as the King's Knot west of the castle was first laid out in this period.

The great hall and the "Foir Front" or screen wall closing off the south side of the main ward were built by James IV, and about that time the Chapel Royal probably originally built by James III was made collegiate. The palace on the south side of the main court was begun by James V in 1538 to house himself and the second of his successive French queens. Queen Mary was crowned as a baby in the Chapel Royal in 1543 and work on the palace and the outer defences is thought to have continued during the regency of her mother, Mary of Guise. As an adult ruler Queen Mary often visited the castle on her way into the Highlands and had a narrow escape on one occasion here when her bed curtains caught fire.

Chapel at Stirling Castle

Fireplace in Stirling Castle

The Palace at Stirling Castle

James VI was christened in the chapel and spent much of his infancy in the castle. In the 1580s he was present when the castle was besieged for a day by its governor the Earl of Mar and the earl of Angus. This was a sequel to the teenage king being seized by several power-hungry nobles in the "Raid of Ruthven" (see page 108), an act for which the Earl of Gowrie was later beheaded for treason below the castle walls. A report of that period suggests that many of the roofs were then in need of repair, and in 1594 the Chapel Royal was entirely rebuilt in great haste for the baptism of Prince Henry. After James succeeded to the English throne in 1603 he paid only two brief visits to Stirling and the castle became little more than a prison for religious nonconformists such as the Earl of Huntly, a catholic held there in 1610-12. Charles I came for two nights in 1633, and in 1650 Charles II stayed briefly in the castle.

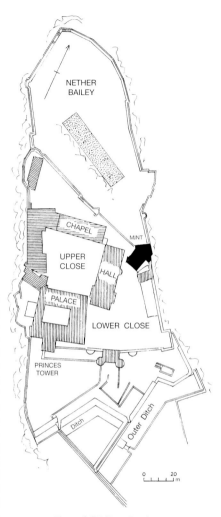

Plan of Stirling Castle

In 1651 the castle was bombarded by Cromwellian forces under General Monk for three days until a mutiny amongst the defenders compelled Colonel William Conyngham to submit. The Earl of Mar's household furnishings and forty pieces of ordnance were amongst the spoils. In 1662 the garrison was said to number about 200 Englishmen. The castle was given back to the keeping of the earls of Mar until George I confiscated it because of Mar's Jacobite sympathies. In the rebellion of 1715 the castle was occupied by General Wightman and the Duke of Argyll, who succeeded in preventing the Jacobites from crossing the Forth, although the battle at Sherriffmuir was indecisive. Prince Charles Edward besieged the castle early in 1746 but General Blakeney held out even after the Prince's victory at Falkirk, and was soon relieved by the Duke of Cumberland. The castle remained in use as a barracks until the 20th century but the state rooms and courtyards have long been open to the public.

On the west side of the town there still survives a substantial length of a town wall built in the 1540s, with one flanking bastion. On the east side of the town much of the wall was demolished in the 1770s. The main area of the castle measures 200m from north to south by 80m wide and is divided into two wards, the northern of which lies at a lower level and now contains only a magazine. An eastern gateway in this ward, and a minor postern elsewhere were both blocked up in the 18th century. Most of the walls are little more than breastworks on top of sheer rock faces and much of them, especially the parapets, are 18th and 19th century, but with 16th and 17th century work incorporated here and there. Towards the more level approach to the SE is a 10m wide dry outer moat flanked at the north end by the Spur Battery, which incorporates a bastion of the 1550s. A gateway in a wall of 1712 admits to a small square and then there is right-angled turn to cross another ditch into another gateway passage through a thick rampart with casemates on the inner side. This gateway (the Overport) has rusticated Tuscan pillars and bears Queen Anne's initials. It pierces the west side of a triangular central bastion which is a work of the 1550s remodelled in 1708-11.

James IV's "Foir Front" of 1500-6 comprised a central gatehouse with drum towers on all four corners, curtain walls with other drum towers on either side not far from the gatehouse, and a four storey rectangular tower at either end. The Prince's Tower adjoining the Palace at the SW end survives complete with a parapet on chequered corbelling with angle-rounds. Only the lower part remains of the Elphinstone Tower at the other end, the Three Gun Battery being built over it. The central gateway passage is flanked by narrower pedestrian gates, each vaulted and once closed by a portcullis. Pit-prisons only reached by hatches lie below guard-rooms in the outer drum towers, which have three levels with dumb-bell shaped gun-loops, but were once probably a storey higher. The inner towers with staircases have been removed. North of the Elphinstone Tower is the Grand Battery of 1689 built over the kitchens, whose vaults were removed and they were then filled with earth. Beyond is the Master Gunner's House also of the 1690s (but with later windows) adjacent to the 16th century Mint built over the north gateway of c1380 to the Nether Bailey. In 1583 the curtain wall west of this gateway was rebuilt after collapsing through lack of maintenance.

Gateway at Stirling Castle

The Great Hall at Stirling lies above cellars in a free-standing harled and embattled block 42m long by 14m wide in the middle of the upper ward. It was divided up to create a barrack block in the 1790s but has now been restored as a splendid single chamber with a new hammerbeam roof based on the old design, mullioned bay windows with looped transoms towards the south end, and several fireplaces. Other windows are placed in a row high up, and have image niches between them. The north end contains the main entrance and was screened off. There are staircase in the corners here, that in the NW corner rising to the musicians gallery and battlements. On the north side of the court west of the hall is the Chapel Royal of 1594 with a symmetrical arrangement of three windows with pairs of round arched lights on either side of a central entrance with twinned columns. Immediately south of it stood the earlier chapel. The apartments west of the court (latterly garrison quarters but now a museum) are largely the work of James IV, but later and possibly earlier work is incorporated, and the north end was rebuilt after a fire in 1855.

James V's Palace on the south side of the court has its own small central court known as the Lion's Den. Above a basement are the king's chambers on the north side and the queen's chambers on the south, with more modest rooms for retainers above. The two main suites each have a large outer hall, a smaller inner hall, a chamber, and smaller private rooms. The two royal bedchambers adjoin each other on the east side. The three facades visible within the castle are faced with high quality ashlar and have parapets with statues set on a heavy cornice. Between the large rectangular windows of the main state rooms furnished with iron grilles are round-headed recesses with cusped heads and classical style statues set on high pedestals carried on huge corbels like human figures. The west range incorporates older work and is narrower than the rest. It was in a collapsing state in the 1580s and only properly repaired in the 1670s. Minor alterations to the palace as a whole were carried out for the Earl of Mar in the early 18th century. Alterations for military usage as barracks in the 19th century, now mostly removed, included a kitchen built against the west side, where there is a small court, and an octagonal latrine in the Lion's Den..

Torwood Castle

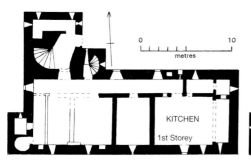

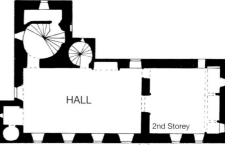

Plans of Torwood Castle

KITCHEN

1st Storey

HALL

2nd Storey

TORWOOD NS 836844 V

There was a older castle here in which Bruce and Comyn met frequently when they were joint Guardians of Scotland. The present ruined L-plan house furnished with oval and diamond-shaped gunloops was built by the Forresters of Garden, keepers of a royal forest here. A stone dated 1566 now lies in Falkland Museum. However recent excavations have shown that parts of the courtyard buildings to the north were older, a block in the NE corner containing a well perhaps being 15th century, whilst there was a round tower on the NW corner. The castle was called Woodhead in 1585 when it was captured by the earls of Angus and Mar with the Master of Glamis. In 1635 Torwood passed to George, Lord Forester of Corstophine and the fireplaces remaining in the west wall of the court may date from his period.

The main block measures 23.2m long by 9m wide and contained a hall and private room over three cellars and a kitchen connected by a passage on the north side. The wing has a wide spiral staircase and a narrower stair in a square turret from the passage continued up to serve the bedrooms, which lay partly in the roof. A third stair lay in another projecting turret at the SW corner. A small room in the wing was latterly inhabited for forty years by a hermit proprietor who slowly and partly restored the east end of the castle, rebuilding much of the kitchen fireplace and putting a concrete vault over the private room, which it would not have had originally. The hall was a fine room with a big fireplace (restored) on the north, and four south-facing windows, the middle two having higher sills to allow for a buffet below them.

Torwood Castle (see also page 3)

TOUCH   NS 753928

Sir Alexander Fraser, a staunch supporter of Robert Bruce, was once laird of Touch, but the present building began as a late 16th century Z-plan mansion erected by the Setons. They were here from the late 15th century until 1930, although a junior branch, the Seton-Steuarts of Allanton, inherited Touch in the mid 18th century. In 1708 the then laird was one of those involved in an abortive Jacobite rebellion who escaped punishment because the trial was mishandled by the Lord Advocate. The west wing is still clearly identifiable as a tower-like structure but the other has been remodelled along with the main block, of which only the north wall now survives. The building has been widened to the north in the 17th century and on the south a splendid Georgian facade added with a central triangular pediment

WOODHEAD   NS 606783

Near the gateway to the mansion of the 1840s called Lennox Castle built by John Kincaid-Lennox is the ivy-clad ruin of a tower measuring 12.6m by 7.6m built by his ancestor John Lennox soon after he succeeded his brother Duncan in 1572.   This branch of the family descended from Donald, son of Duncan, 8th Earl of Lennox. Their seat was at Balcorrach from 1421 until Woodhead was built. A shield on the south side bears his arms and those of his wife, one of the Cuninghams. The upper parts are very ruined as a result of partial demolition of the then habitable building in the 1840s, after which the basement was used for a while rather unsuccessfully as an ice-house. This basement contained a kitchen and cellar linked by a passage on the south side to a stair in a small wing at the SW corner. At a later date the wing was demolished and a much wider staircase built in this position. In the original re-entrant angle was a turret stair from the hall to the bedrooms. Except for one north window, a room in the NW corner beside the kitchen fireplace flue, and a NE aumbry, the features of the hall are all later insertions.

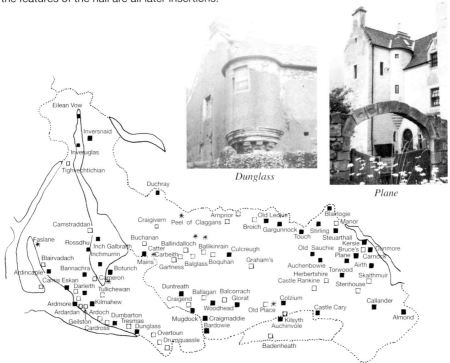

Dunglass

Plane

Touch House

Touch House

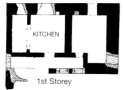

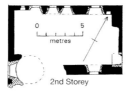

Plans of Woodhead

Plan of Touch House

OTHER FORMER CASTLES IN DUNBARTONSHIRE & STIRLINGSHIRE

ARDARDAN NS 331785 Site of tower of Noble family.

ARDOCH NS 364768 Site of castle of the Bontine family.

ARDOCH NS 412864 Site of castle of the Findlay family.

ARNPRIOR NS 615943 Nothing now remains of the castle of the Buchanans

BALCASTLE NS 701782 Motte rising above stream to summit measuring 36m by 26m.

BLAIRHENECHAN NS 338792 18th and 19th century Drumhead House may lie on site.

BLAIRVADACH NS 263853 House on site of castle of MacAulays of Ardincaple.

BONNYBRIDGE NS 824798 Motte 3.3m high, 30m by 21m at base. By Antoinine wall.

BROICH NS 641951 House demolished in 1852 had defensive ditch and rampart.

CAMSTRADDAN NS 359922 Colquhoun castle on former island replaced by house in 1739

CASTLEHILL or CARDROSS NS 385757 Site of house where Robert Bruce died in 1329.

CRAIGEND NS 545778 Demolished mansion of 1812 incorporated older parts.

DRUMQUASSLE NS 515710 Site of castle of the Cunninghams.

FASLANE NS 257878 Earthworks of castle of Earl of Lennox where Wallace took refuge.

GARCHELL NS 548948 Low mound once 25m square to NE of farmhouse.

GARTFERRAN NS 538953 Rampart and ditch around platform about 50m by 45m.

GLENTIRRAN NS 668944 Former Livingstone house, passed to Campbells 18th century.

GRANGE NT 015815 Site of Hamilton tower altered by Cadells in 19th century.

KARIG LION NS 987812 Site of dower house of Lyon family later occupied by steelworks.

KEPPOCH NS 330798 Mansion of 1820 on or near site of castle of Stirlings of Glorat.

OLD BALLINKINRAIN NS 561880 17th century building within later mansion. Napier seat.

OLD PLACE NS 690778 Site of castle of Livingstones of Kilsyth. It was ruinous by 1740.

OVERTOUN NS 424761 Mid 19th century mansion on site of castle.

POLMAISE NS 835924 Site of Cunningham mansion of 1691 on site of older building.

TIGHVECHTICHAN NN 312045 Site of a castle of the MacFarlanes.

TRESMAS NS 428753 Remains of a Colquhoun castle survived until early 19th century.

TULLICHEWAN NS 382815 Demolished 1954. Fragments of walled garden remain.

INDEX OF CASTLES AND CASTELLATED HOUSES